John G. Lake's

Writings

— From —

Africa

Includes Previously
Unpublished Writings

Compiled by Rev. Curry R. Blake

Published by:

CHRISTIAN REALITY BOOKS

P.O. Box 742947

Dallas TX 75374

1-888-293-6591

Cover Design by CBC Creative.

Unless otherwise noted, all Scripture quotations are taken from the King James Bible.

ISBN 978-0-9892305-7-5

Printed in the United States of America.

REV18122014

TABLE OF CONTENTS

PREFACE 1

UNPUBLISHED WRITINGS FROM SOUTH AFRICA 5

THE APOSTOLIC FAITH 7

"THE UPPER ROOM" LETTERS JUNE 1909................................. 9

"THE UPPER ROOM" LETTERS MAY 1910 23

HOW GOD MAKES MISSIONARIES.......................................27

REPORTS FROM REGIONS BEYOND 33

LETTER FROM SOUTH AFRICA 37

NEWS FROM SOUTH AFRICA..43

A CALL FOR HELPERS 49

"THE UPPER ROOM" LETTERS AUGUST 1909.........................53

THE POSITION OF THE APOSTOLIC FAITH 57

    The Patriarchal Dispensation 58

    The Mosaic Dispensation....................................58

    The Christian Dispensation 59

    Paul's Warnings..60

    The Lord Jesus Raises the Standard for the Christian

    Dispensation 60

    The Great Debate 61

    The New Covenant 63

    The Sabbath Day 64

    An Apt Illustration...65

    Our High Christian Privilege 66

    The First Day...68

"THE UPPER ROOM" LETTERS NOVEMBER 1910......................69

"THE UPPER ROOM" LETTERS OCTOBER 1910 73

IN JOHANNESBURG..79

GOD IS STILL WORKING MIGHTILY.. 85

LATEST NEWS FROM AFRICA DECEMBER 1908 95

AN EDUCATION IN FAITH 97

ASLEEP IN JESUS... 99

"THE UPPER ROOM" LETTERS OCTOBER 1909 105

"THE UPPER ROOM" UPDATES.. 107

GOD'S MIGHTY MOVINGS IN AFRICA 109

MORE NEWS FROM SOUTH AFRICA................................... 113

    The Compound Work 118

    A Word of Warning.. 119

SANCTIFICATION AND HOLY LIVING 123

SOUTH AFRICA AND BROTHER LAKE.............................. 129

THE AFRICAN DIARY OF JOHN G. LAKE........................ 135

    Forward.. 137

BAPTIZED IN THE HOLY GHOST...................................... 139

DIARY ENTRIES NOV. 24, 1910 – JAN. 2, 1911 151

THE HISTORY OF JOHN G. LAKE HEALING ROOMS................ 189

Preface

John G. Lake lived from 1870 until 1935. His entire family received the benefit of divine healing through the ministry of John Alexander Dowie. In 1901, Lake moved his family to Zion, IL, where he served as Dowie's Building Manager until 1904 when he moved his family back to Chicago. Lake stayed in Chicago running an insurance company for a group of entrepreneurs.

In 1907, Charles F. Parham held Pentecostal meetings in Zion in F. F. Bosworth's home (because the religious leaders in Zion would not allow Parham to erect his tent or rent suitable facilities for the meetings).

Bosworth received the Baptism with the Holy Spirit with speaking in tongues along with several others who were promptly dis-fellowshipped.

In Oct. 1907, Lake received the Holy Spirit Baptism while visiting a sick woman with F.F. Bosworth and Tom Hezmelhalch. Lake immediately distributed his finances and personal belongings and began preparing to go to South Africa as a missionary. Within six months after receiving the Holy Spirit Baptism, Lake was in South Africa. This decisiveness characterized Lake's entire life and ministry.

Lake's wife died only six months after their arrival in South Africa. There have been many theories set forth as to the cause of her death. This is not the time or place to discuss the evidence I have found. (I will do that in a later volume.) John remained in South Africa for another four and one half years, returning to the U.S. permanently on Feb. 1, 1913.

In 1914, after attending the founding of the Assemblies of God in Hot Springs, he went to England where he founded his own organization called "The International Apostolic Council." He desired to see this organization serve as a return to the original "Apostolic" power and purpose of the waning Pentecostal movement.

John then moved to Spokane, WA, with a new wife, Florence, and five children from his first wife. There Dr. Lake started several other organizations including "Lake's Healing Rooms," "John G. Lake's Divine Healing Institute," and his church which went by several names including "Lake's Apostolic Tabernacle" and "The Church at Spokane." Lake lived in Spokane from September 1914 until May 1920 when he moved to Portland, OR.

When Dr. Lake moved from Spokane to Portland, he closed his famous "Healing Rooms" and opened new Healing Rooms in Portland. He remained in Portland for five years before beginning a missionary church planting tour of California and Texas, opening churches in San

Diego, Sacramento, and Houston. Dr. Lake moved back to Spokane in 1931, where he lived until his death in 1935. After his final move to Spokane, he opened Healing Rooms in his church at Main and Lincoln.

He never reopened Healing Rooms in any other buildings and the original building burned and was torn down and replaced by an entirely different building with different floor levels and building orientation.

Wilford Reidt, Dr. Lake's son-in-law, carried the ministry until shortly before his death in June of 1987. Before his passing, he named Rev. Curry R. Blake as the General Overseer of The International Apostolic Council (aka: John G. Lake Ministries). Using a manual of Dr. Lake's that was given to him by a Divine Healing Technician who had been trained personally by Dr. Lake, Rev. Blake has begun training and certifying Divine Healing Technicians.

Rev. Blake has now trained over 100,000 DHT's and has testimonies of thousands of healings of every kind of disease including several instances of the dead being raised.

The writings in this book were from or about John G. Lake during his time as a Missionary to South Africa from 1908 until 1913.

We have also included the transcripts of Dr. Lake's personal diary dating from 1908 until 1911. You will read Lake's own account of the tremendous revival that started when a band of 12 missionaries (including the family members) arrived in South Africa.

Each entry in this book is completely unedited and is exactly as it was originally written by Dr. Lake and various others. Since it is an unedited document, you may notice some missing text or lines where text was illegible.

John G. Lake Ministries may be contacted at:

JOHN G. LAKE MINISTRIES

P.O. Box 742947

Dallas, TX. 75374

1-888-293-6591

www.jglm.org

JOHN G. LAKE'S

UNPUBLISHED WRITINGS FROM SOUTH AFRICA

1908 - 1913

THE
APOSTOLIC FAITH

JOHANNESBURG, AFRICA
OCTOBER 1908

Oh! I wish more of our people were here, you have never seen such a land of opportunity, and people's hearts are receptive – they are hungry – there has never been a real pungent revival in Africa that has at all touched the populace and our faith goes out to God and we want your prayers to this end, that not only a little local revival, but a mighty outpouring of God's Spirit upon the whole land shall come.

Hold us before God; we need your prayers, we need them mightily. Your brother in Jesus till He comes,

John G. Lake

"THE UPPER ROOM" LETTERS
JUNE 1909

PUBLISHED IN "THE UPPER ROOM" NEWSLETTER JUNE 1909

The second letter is from Brother John G. Lake, which he asks us to publish and other Pentecostal papers to copy. In it he describes the state of affairs in South Africa, financially and otherwise. He issues a strong warning against missionaries rushing out there from America or England except under certain conditions mentioned. He mentions the difficulty, which attended the landing of our dear Brother Schwede, who used to worship with us in the Upper Room. The difficulty arose through his not having $100 which is required of all who go to the Transvaal colony. Here is what Brother Lake says:

You see, these African states are independent governments – Cape Colony, Natal, Orange Free State and the Transvaal. Consequently, a missionary who is coming to Johannesburg must be qualified under the Transvaal law, which is – that every immigrant (missionary or otherwise) shall possess $100 before he is permitted to land – that he must show that he has some employment in view in case he is a laborer or business man, and that if he is a missionary he must show that he is receiving support from America, so that he is not likely to become a charge on the government or in other words, a pauper.

Now, there seems to be a misconception in America that I want to have righted. First, Apostolic Faith Missionaries, or any kind of Faith Missionaries, are not welcomed by the government in Africa – no missionary who is looking for his support from this land is wanted by the government here. If he can show that he is being supported by some organized body in the homeland, it is all well, but it is perfectly natural that Africa should not care to be burdened with great numbers of missionaries who expect to get their existence from the people here.

This land is just recovering from a great war, which has utterly devastated the country. Everything that could be burned was burned and the cattle were killed, simply to cut off the food supply from the Boers in order to end the war. The result is this country is in a very hard plight financially, and will be for a good many years to come. It is like the South in America was at the close of the Civil War.

This matter of Brother Schwede being short of funds gave us a great deal of trouble and expense. Personally, I spent almost an entire week and $10 of money in connection with telegraphing and otherwise in our endeavor to get him through. Finally, through the American Consulate here, we succeeded in obtaining permission from the Transvaal government to let him come to Johannesburg. Then when he landed we found that he did not have money sufficient to pay his fare here. We were then compelled to send him $22.50 for his carfare, which was, among this bunch of missionaries, a mighty big sum to raise.

In the first place, the American missionaries should not run over here until they know what they are doing, and under what conditions they can be received; and that they first correspond with us and let us know who they are, because we have got to make representation to the government concerning them before they land. Now, it chanced that Brother Schwede's mail from America arrived in advance of himself, and we were compelled to open his mail in order to identify him and know anything about him. After this, if there are any more missionaries coming we want to know who they are in advance – we want to know their character and the kind of workers they are – otherwise we cannot make any more representations concerning people we do not know.

The government holds us responsible for Apostolic Faith Missionaries arriving in Africa. It is all right for Apostolic Faith Missionaries to run around free handed in America, because they are on their own land – everybody understands them and knows their purpose and their teaching. We are in a strange land, and under different laws, and we have got to comply with governmental regulations here, and the government keeps us under close scrutiny all the time, the same as it does with all other missionaries; and further, the Word of God demands that we comply with their laws.

Now, brethren, another thing. Brother Schwede is here on the ground. He is a precious man. We welcome him with all our soul. We are glad he has come, but brethren, I feel that the American people must take care of Brother Schwede now since he is on the field. Considering everything, living here is about twice as high or expensive as it is in America, while some things are no dearer than in America, yet other things are so extremely high. The home in which we live (17 of us live in five rooms) rents for $40 per month. God has given us this home free of rent in answer to prayer, or otherwise I do not know what we would do. It has been a very hard matter to exist here.

In a whole year, since leaving America, all the American money that I have received was $29 from United States of America, and recently, since my wife's death, a lady in Canada sent us $26 as a Christmas gift to my wife, which arrived here after she was dead. There have been many days when the larder was low, and there have been many times when we ate our breakfast that there was nothing left for dinner. We started to live on the food that the African people are accustomed to living on here, but finally decided that it was not wise.

We are not accustomed to this kind of living. This is a hot climate, different from what we have been accustomed to and we are not acclimated and so we simply had to live as we had been accustomed to in America. Otherwise, probably we would have all died. When the other missionaries had begun to arrive I urged them to live as they had been accustomed to in America – people cannot change their manner of life in this respect.

I have a feeling that this party of African missionaries have had very little attention given them by the people in the homeland. It is beautiful to talk and say nice things concerning missions and missionaries, but when you are in the field under the boiling sun of Africa, with an empty stomach, it is then that you will find out the kind of goods that the Lord has put in your soul – it is so much different than from shouting in meetings after coming from a good supper. God has done marvelous things in the way of the extension of the Gospel.

We have a tremendous native work on our hands, and we heartily welcome REAL MISSIONARIES, but they cannot come to Africa with the thought of a lot of "brand new American ideas" to teach to the natives. One of the curses of American missionaries is that when they come here they forthwith are teaching social equality between the white people and the natives.

Now, the African native is a very different man from the American Negro. The African man is a heathen – he does not wear anything but a blanket until he is taught and Christianized. Missionaries coming to this land must be prepared to come and learn, and in these days when God is calling men out into the missionary field, they want to come in wisdom and strength and knowledge, too. I know that the American people have not had a chance to understand conditions here, nor have we the opportunity to lay before the American people the conditions as they are here.

We do it as rapidly as possible, but it is slow in process through a letter on notation. But one thing must be stopped once and for all, and that is, all kinds of missionaries running out to Africa before they understand what conditions are here, and how to get here; you will learn how to get here at the close of this letter; otherwise, when they land at Cape Town they will simply be compelled to go back again and not be permitted to land.

We earnestly trust the dear people of America will take upon their souls the burdens of this work, this mighty work of God, and pray down the funds with which to extend the Kingdom of God in Africa. God has used us in a marvelous way, and many wonderful doors have been opened and are being opened.

14

At this present time, it is not so much the question of getting missionaries here as the funds with which to put missionaries that are here, on the field. We have men here far superior to any that can come from America. Among the baptized people are men who can speak English, Dutch, Zulu, Basuto and other languages. The American missionary coming out here has got all these to learn, if he is to be an effective worker.

Of course, there is room for some kind of missionaries, especially strong preachers, who can take representative, work in a city and conduct it, but these are not usually the men that we find as ordinary missionaries. We also need good, strong Bible teachers, who are rooted and grounded and established in the Word of God to teach the young missionaries that God is raising up here.

In time to come, there will be a demand for the ordinary missionary from America, which will only be after the American people have financed this proposition and the situation is on a solid footing and the thing put in working order in a broader way – then missionaries can be stationed in the different fields and cared for – otherwise the thing will be a failure.

Concerning our strong men here: We have one white overseer with about 35 native under-preachers (with 10,000 adherents in one locality), and up to the present time we have not been able to give this man one cent. Brethren, these things ought not to be so. If God has called this man (he is a man baptized in the Holy Ghost) with a wife and six children to give their lives and endure hardships on the field for the spread of the Gospel amongst the black people of Africa, I am pretty sure He has called somebody in America to furnish him a decent living while he does it.

This dear brother's name is P. E. LeRoux, an Africander (i.e., a white man born here), speaking Dutch and English and at least two native languages, thoroughly accustomed with native affairs, who is worth as much in the extension of the Kingdom of God as twenty American missionaries would be. We have also another native work, with about fifty native preachers, that has recently come into our hands, and we need a strong, clear-headed Africander who understands the natives and their customs, etc., to oversee this work; and bless God we have got the man, but we have not got the funds with which to send him on the field and keep him alive after he gets there.

Fifty dollars per month would do for this man and his family, and that would mean the taking care of a native work touching 35,000 people. We have another brother, a real Moody among the natives, who must have at once $1000 in order to equip his work so that his fifty native under-preachers with established works may be touched by himself (every congregation) once in a year at least.

God has done such marvelous things in this way of opening up doors for us that we can hardly realize it ourselves; but if this work of God is to go forward, it can only be through the self-sacrifice of those in the homeland who have properties and money that should be devoted and consecrated to the extension of this work of God. There are only one million white people in South Africa, and the very small percentage of these are real Christians, who live in a poor land.

There is not the wealth here that there is in America, except the money-makers, if I may use that term, in the mining district, who are unsaved people and care little about the work of God. The Dutch people live here very simply and plainly; indeed, one family was compelled to live for many months on nothing but corn meal, and many of these Dutch families do this. If an American family was compelled to do this they would consider it a great hardship.

The natives live on corn meal mush, absolutely, without salt or sugar, except in rare cases. It will cost Brother Schwede $1 for a meal, or $21.60 per month to board at a restaurant. You cannot rent a decent room here for less than $10 per month – most all rent for $15 per month, furnished or unfurnished, no difference; but we feel that we might be able to secure him room rent and boarding for less money than the above-stated with some of our sacrificing Pentecostal people here. But, brethren, our Pentecostal people here are not rich, and

17

we know that the Lord will direct Brother Schwede where to put his money which comes in over and above enough to support himself.

Another party of missionaries who have been baptized since we came here are going into Central Africa. In order to get to their field they must have three African mountain wagons, with eight pairs of donkeys for each wagon. This party will go over land from Johannesburg to Victoria Falls, and beyond there. If you will look this up on the map you will see what a vast country they will have to cover to get there. They cannot travel in the heat of the day, as the sun is too hot.

Their three outfits will cost $1000; yet, if I were to say to you that probably as in proportion in some cases, 100,000 might be saved through this effort (this would be 1 cent apiece for the salvation of their souls) you would hardly believe it. Brethren, join us in prayer that God will open the door and help us out in some of these tremendous problems.

God is doing marvelous things amongst the native people. These men and women get saved and get healed, and they have faith in God for the salvation and the healing of others. It goes from one to another like wildfire – it is the ministry of healing that carries the gospel. Missionaries without faith for healing do not amount to much in this country – there are plenty of them here now who scarcely touch the people. The ministry of healing has taken the gospel into many quarters with a rapidity that we have never before known. One brother, who has the oversight of 25,000 practically touching with his influence 50,000 natives, commenced his work four years ago, alone, himself and his wife. This brother knows God for healing, which God has used to make his work what it is.

Beloved, do take this burden on your souls. We must have help. It is almost torture to look about and see the doors that God has opened, and we are not able to touch simply on account of a few dollars. One dear native who has had a wonderful ministry in the salvation and healing of his people came to my home last night and simply begged for $50 with which to pay the transportation of his wood and iron church that the natives now own, which has to be removed and taken to another locality and set up.

This church has got to be removed by July. Brother Schwede, myself and Brother Vandewal, one of our strong Dutch preachers, were simply unable to refuse this man his request, and as we got down and prayed we pledged him that on June 15 we would get him this $50. Some how, brethren the Lord God has got to find it – it is not in our crowd.

The poverty amongst the white people in this land is very intense – you cannot keep a shilling in your pocket when you meet hungry women and children every day.

These conditions here are adjusting themselves very gradually, but it is only a short time since the Boer War closed, and the people have not had time yet to get themselves homes and commence to live decent, and labor for white men is very scarce. The mines are operated almost entirely by native labor. White men are only employed to oversee, etc. Brethren, you must take this burden on your hearts, we cannot carry it – it is too great for us.

Brother Schwede, myself and others have been in prayer over this thing and in particularly during the last two days, and I have a conviction in my soul that the American people are going to raise up and take advantage of these marvelous opportunities, and that the people at home are going to catch the spirit of self-sacrifice for Jesus Christ the same as those who have come from the land and are now on the field.

Again, concerning Brother Schwede. He had plenty of money and more than he needed to get to Africa. If it had been wisely expended, he could have landed here at Johannesburg with $100 in his pocket, and perhaps that $100 would have save a thousand souls here. Brethren these are serious matters, and wisdom from God needs to be used. We have got to make God's money go as far for Him, as we would for a businessman or like the world does, to accomplish their plans.

So this is the reason that I urge once more that the people intending to come to Africa must make themselves familiar with circumstances, and we would prefer that they correspond with us in advance, as missionaries before leaving America should have one of our missionary certificates or a letter from us in order to land at Cape Town, because we are now recognized as the Apostolic Missionary Board here by the government, and are being held responsible for all missionaries of like precious faith by them. These certificates or letters would be their credentials for admission into the country.

Only once more. Every individual, upon arriving at Cape Town, must possess $100, missionary or no missionary. If a man is the head of a family and has a wife and children, he must possess $100 at least, or more; $100 is the minimum. I believe they will admit most any man with a family if he has $100, but in such cases it is better to have more, especially if some are of age. Brother Schwede tells me that there were more men, women and children who came on the ship he did, who were simply compelled to return to England and were not permitted to land at all, and I feel that it was only on account of the interference of God on his behalf that got him through. I am under bond to the American consulate and to the government at Pretoria to see that he does not become a charge on the public.

Consequently you are aware of the condition we are placed in here, and I know that you dear people will do all you can concerning him and his work. This is a mighty work. I do not believe that there has been in modern days anything like this work anywhere in real effectiveness – in real salvation, sanctification, healing and baptizing of people. But it is only in its infancy.

We earnestly pray that you will unite in prayer with us in behalf of this thing and everything else in connection with the work here, that the mighty power of God will rest upon us, that we shall keep under the precious blood and humble at the feet of Jesus, where He may continue to use us. Otherwise, even after He has used us, we may become castaways.

Your brother, in Jesus' name,

John G. Lake

"THE UPPER ROOM" LETTERS MAY 1910

PUBLISHED IN "THE UPPER ROOM" NEWSLETTER MAY 1910

Written: April 2nd, 1910, South Africa

Praise GOD, the work is moving on in South Africa, moving rapidly, for God is at the back of it. We have just received the following items of news in a letter from Brother J. G. Lake dated April 2nd.

I am having some preliminary native conferences, one yesterday at Kretzschmar offices, one today at my home, and on Monday we will have a full day of it. These are all preliminary for the big conference. Bloemfontein begins next week Thursday.

This week Kretzschmar presented news with a letter giving facts concerning the work in the Free State, including a list of congregations, and reports 16,000 people actually in our hands in the Free State. That don't mean, brother, that the district in which we minister has 16,000 people but means that we are ministering regularly to 16,000 people that comprise our congregations in the Free State alone.

In a conference yesterday, a Presbyterian native minister at Droonstadt made application to be received into our native ministry. He comes with an entire congregation and under our arrangement instead of just ministering to his present congregation, we sent our native evangelists into that district and will congregate 10 to 15 congregations over which he shall act as a sort of district evangelist. We largely follow the form the old Methodist church in systematizing our work.

The native work has become a mighty tremendous problem, how to keep it moving without permitting it to decline in Spirit and power is the great question at hand. We have not been able to keep white workers among the natives as we should for sometime for lack of funds. Brother Le Roux was just returned from the Free State where we conducted services for some weeks reporting a mighty aggressive work among the natives there with real God-power.

Yesterday in our conference at Kretzschmar's office a white brother came in. A manufacturer who probably had come from [the town of] Kretzschmar to pray for him. He asked that we pray for him. Instead of Brother Kretzschmar and I praying for him, we invited the native brethren to pray for him.

Three of them stepped forward and laid their hands on him and, like a flash from heaven, God healed him. These men are crude and many things in their lives do not appeal to us as the right thing at all times. Frequently we have to deal with them strongly and clearly and exercise a good deal of discipline to keep them out of sin: for the native is still a child-man though he is saved and, like a child, it is easy for him to fall back into sin.

Nevertheless, you show them, brother, that God honors them. I wish that the dear Christians could have some practical experience among natives. It would destroy a lot of their ideas that a native has when saved is instantly transformed into the ideal Christian character that we build up in our minds. He is just an animal and the animal in him predominates. Given the submergence of the animal comes gradually as the Spirit of God in him is permitted to develop and obtain power over him.

We had a wonderful testimony meeting the other night in which some testimonies of real miracles were given. I wish I could send you some at this writing. In a postscript written from Bloemfontein from Orange River colony, he says: "Here are some official statistics of our work. We have in South Africa 250 native preachers from all grades and 100 white preachers from all grades. Since our return to Africa, God has given us 100 new native preachers. These are the official conference reports.

A brother Lesheka, with 65 local preachers and 4000 people, were received into this mission at this conference. What open doors! What open doors! Oh, do pray for God's mighty power to save."

John G. Lake

HOW GOD MAKES MISSIONARIES

The story of a conversion, sanctification, baptism in the Holy Ghost and a call to preach.

In the Congregation at Johannesburg one evening. A young lady said to me, "That young gentleman, Mr. Kretzschmar, sitting near the pillar is a friend of mine." In a few words she told me a little of his life and present condition – an educated infidel, far away from God, a student of Bradlaw, Ingersol. Payne, Voltaire and other infidel writers. A man of broad spirit and large heart and said she, "A company of us have been earnestly praying to God to save him, and we feel, brother, that if you will join us in prayer, God will save him soon." I replied, "Let us pray that God will save him tonight."

At the close of the service, one of our workers, Brother John Armstrong, in company with the lady who is now his wife, Miss Kidson, shook hands with Kretzschmar in the aisle of the church, at the same time inviting him to walk with them toward the home where they were stopping. On arriving, they sat conversing until about two o'clock in the morning. Mr. Armstrong said, "It is too late for you to go home, Gerald.

Remain with us, but before retiring it is our custom to have prayer. Will you kneel with us while we pray? Kretzschamar replied, "It is your home and it is your custom to pray. I will kneel, not in acknowledgement of your God, but because I am a gentleman, and I am in your home." They knelt and prayed.

Brother Kretzschmar said, in relating this incident to the congregation at Johannesburg, "Three minutes after I knelt to pray, I was seized by some mighty power that I could not comprehend. Being a student of psychology and being familiar with many phases of psychological manifestations, I said to myself. "What psychological force is this that has got hold of me with such dreadful power? I yield to no psychical force."

He shut his teeth, and for two hours battled, as he said, like a bulldog, until the sweat poured down his body. At the end of two hours of this terrific struggle, the Spirit of the Lord said to him, "Why do you fight? I am Jesus. I have come to baptize you with the Holy Ghost." Instantly I said, "Jesus, if this is You, I surrender to You, but I surrender to no other power." He said, "In one minute I was speaking in tongues and the glory and power of God filled my soul."

This young man was familiar with the English, Dutch, Zulu and Basuto languages, and has passed a successful civil service examination in them. The Lord at once called him to preach the Gospel, and the mighty power of God has followed his ministry. Hundreds and hundreds have been saved under the preaching of the Everlasting Gospel of the Son of God through this brother.

The latest official report of the African work dated November 22, 1909, speaking of the work in Orange River Colony says, "Orange River Colony. Brother John G. Lake and others labored here for a while, and Brother Gerald Kretzschmar is now in charge of the work. The Government was given recognition of our work. Centers of the work have been established at Bloemfontein, Heilbron, Frankfort, Lindley, Leuw Bank, Ladybrand, etc. Several native preachers are engaged in the work and a few white brethren.

In writing of the work in the Orange River Colony, South Africa, under date of August 27, 1909, Kretzschmar says, "Brother Lake, personally I have not been through one-quarter of the work in Orange River Colony. It is one of the most gigantic fields that I know of. You will understand me when I say that it is from one extreme end to the other extreme end of the Colony and through the center. The places that I have not been near are as follows: Bethulie, Jacobsthal, De Wetsdorp, Maseru (just on the border of Basutoland and Orange River Colony); Ladybrand, Ficksburg, Bloemfontein, Kroonstad, Senekel Hoopstad, Bothaville, Wolverhook, Viljoensdrift, Villiersdorp."

Brother Kretzschmar continues as follows:

"I have just named the towns in which we have an actual work going on among the native people. Of course each town has a very large district, and in each district we have hundreds and hundreds of people, and I assure you without a word of exaggeration that people are constantly being added to the number.

All the places above mentioned, until the time of writing you, no white missioner has yet visited, and you know sufficient about the work in the Orange River Colony to warrant the statement that, should a white missioner actually visit these places, it is certain that where I give you figures in hundreds now, there I would be able to give you figures in thousands – yes, tens of thousands. This mission is one that is going to consolidate the native people of Africa into one huge nation – in obedience to JESUS and His Word, I believe.

Further, the Apostolic Faith Mission is the actual instrument in God's hand to avert one of the most bloody wars, known only to those who are laboring actually among the natives. Whole Kraals – yes whole Kraals – have gone down like wax candles before the furnace of His Divine Word. I will here mention two instances One Kraal was that at a farm called Green Vlei. We preached here on the 8th of August, 1909, and captured the whole – lock, stock and barrel – and ended up by baptizing every one of them. And the second

Kraal was at a farm called Reikil. Here Jesus actually captured a large number of Dutch people and the whole native Kraal. And at these two places, persecution has done much to consolidate the people to Jesus and our Mission.

At the place called Green Vlei we were almost murdered. They got hold of me and at one time there were actually nine fists in my face; but, glory be to Jesus, not one of them touched me. Had those people a gun, they would have shot me forthwith. Here the native people begged me to allow them to fight these men; but I had such control over them that a word was enough. I gave them the command to turn the other cheek and they obeyed like lambs. At this place we had a big baptismal service in the presence of our enemies, and God broke them down until they came and asked me to forgive them, and expressed their sorrow. Truly the persecution did much to cement these people to Jesus.

"I could go on for hours telling you of this wonderful work brought about by the Gospel of our Lord and Savior." The official report of the work in Africa in peaking of the work in Basutoland says:

"Basutoland: Brother Kretzschmar began a most blessed ministry among the natives last month. Over 250,000 natives live here under British protection. It is their own country. The Chief and people gladly received the teaching wherever the brethren went, and some fifty have been baptized in the Holy Ghost. Brothers F. Schoorbe and P. Van der Merse have also been working there, and are returning there this week. A few centers have been established and native workers called."

Brother Kretzschmar further writes: "My feet have been sore and blistered with tramping hundreds of miles over these hills and mountains, my body weary and worn, and my tongue parched under this burning sun. I have been compelled to tramp on foot because we cannot afford to hire a cart or horses. Pray for me, Brother."

To which Brother Lake replied: "I am not sorry that your body has been weary and your feet sore; mine have been many times, and that for the devil. We can have sore feet and weary bodies just as well as our Lord, and a good deal better. Nevertheless, God is going to let us have things {illegible} than they are now. But the people will be able to appreciate and get the {illegible} out of a victory, are those who have the plodding and the pounding, with cuffs and sleeves up in the early stages of work as it is now. God bless you. Go on!! God has put the tiger in you, let Him govern the tiger, and it will be all right."

John G. Lake

REPORTS FROM REGIONS BEYOND

Written: January 1909

Dear Sister Smock,

I want to make this letter strictly business. Johannesburg is unquestionably the greatest field for missionary effort in the known world. In the last three or four years, the natives from the very interior of Africa are now coming up to Johannesburg to work in the mines. They live in the compounds, and on Sunday afternoon you can address 2,500 natives in most of the compounds, and there are over 500 compounds.

The actual native compound population being two hundred and fifty thousand scattered along the railway at the various mines for 50 miles. What is on my soul is this that some of these dear souls who have been waiting and preparing and praying and praying and apparently getting nowhere, get into God's order of getting things from God and come as God called them, and commence to use the faith they have got, and as they use it, they will get more. You know what a fight it was on my part to believe God for ordinary healings from God.

You know that how as we kept at His feet and prayed there and continued to believe Him, that even while in our effort there was much of self manifest, and the intensity of desire and determination to believe God was taken by many for mere self-effort. The result has been that at the end of one year and three months since we commenced to read Mark 11:22-26 that God as made it so real to us that every day now we witness marvelous healings and, in fact, I do not hesitate to say that 90 persons out of every 100 with whom we pray have been healed, and I believe 75 percent of these have been healed instantaneously.

On Wednesday at a cottage meeting, there was a paralyzed girl brought in in a wheelchair. Her name was Flossie Rens. Her address 25 Kimberley Road, Bertrams, Johannesburg. She had not stood on her feet for seven years. Her mother was a widow and very poor. Mrs. Lake and I prayed for her, asking God to cause the infirm devil to come out of her and deliver her right there. When we ceased praying, I took her by the hand and said to her, "Sister, in the name of God, get up."

At first she hesitated, but I assured her that God had done the work, and immediately she arose, took my arm and we walked 200 feet. Her deliverance was absolute and entire, and aside from the fact that her limbs were withered and undeveloped for lack of use for 7 years, she is just as she was before she was sick.

A young man came last night who had a worm in his foot. He had been prayed with at one of the meetings a month ago. This worm was in the flesh and wound itself round and round the foot. I have forgotten the name of the worm. I have never heard of anything of the kind before. It seemed to be something peculiar in Africa. He had been treated by all the prominent physicians in the largest cities of Africa, and had been to Europe to specialists there. No hope could be given him, all medical aid had failed. As we prayed with him we commanded in the name of Jesus that the thing should die and cease to be. He said last night the thing is absolutely gone and he is perfectly healed, and he had never felt the thing from the moment we prayed. His foot is just like the other one. I mention these simply as an example of what God is doing. Instantaneous healings used to be the exception; today they are the rule.

God is doing wonderful work here. I cannot tell you what wonderful manifestations of the Spirit of God that we see every day in depth and character, a hundred times beyond anything I have ever witnessed in America. The work here is the most spiritual I have ever seen anywhere, but there is such a demand for workers today. I could place a hundred workers today, if they were only here. Dear Sister, in Jesus' name, do get a hold on some of the home people and get them into clearer light and real faith in God, and believe God for coming here.

There are fifty thousand Chinese here. They live in compounds, too. The Chinese missionary from Canton, who ministers to them, was baptized with the Holy Ghost last night. He is a precious fellow. One of the Baker missionaries, Brother Ingram has received his baptism. A Dutch missionary, next door to where we live, Mr. VanMerlie, has received his baptism.

I do have it in my soul that God wants to shake up some of the people in America who have calls and get them out here. Those who are wondering about where they are called to. If they have got a call anywhere, God can use them here. There are hundreds of thousands of Mohammedans and natives of India all over Africa. And if they have got a call to India, this is India enough. If they have got a call to China, this is China enough.

John G. Lake

Johannesburg, South Africa

LETTER FROM SOUTH AFRICA

Missionary Faith Home

Johannesburg, South Africa

Written: April 1, 1909

In order that you may have a better understanding of what the Lord is doing here I will say that in the past fifteen days we have been asked to become overseers of thirty-five thousand native people and five thousand Dutch and German, in one locality, in giving them divine guidance and direction (these five thousand are in German South West Africa), which with the people that we ordinarily touch in the progress of the work in Johannesburg, Pretoria, Krugersdorp, Venoni, Germiston, Durban, Vryheid, and many other places too numerous to mention, makes at least fifty thousand who are now looking to us for divine guidance and direction in the Word of God.

From one of the branch works at Vrededorp, eighteen candidates came for baptism by immersion at our central Tabernacle service last Lord's day. From this same branch hundreds of conversions and hundreds of healings, besides many being sanctified through the precious blood and baptized in the Holy Ghost, have been reported.

Some of the most miraculous healings I have ever beheld have been at this branch. A brother who is in charge of this branch was a young Salvation Army worker for some time. He was not considered a profitable worker, and was finally dropped from the Army's list. However, he was a godly man. In company with a wife and two children, he came from Cape Town here, sought God for the baptism of the Holy Ghost, and the Lord baptized him in the Tabernacle following one of the evening services.

After the Lord baptized him and spoke through him in tongues, he came to me saying, "Brother Lake, I am troubled about my wife. She has not been making the progress in God that I have; I am anxious that we should move together and be one in the experience of the baptism, as we have been in almost everything else." I said, "All right, brother, let us pray now." In company with some other saints we knelt on the floor and asked God to baptize her then and there. She was at a friend's house, four miles away.

In a short time he returned home, and found upon his arrival that the very moment we had prayed, the power of God had descended on his wife while she was lying in her bed, and as he approached her bedside, to his own astonishment he found that she was praising God in tongues. This young Dutchman speaks both English and Dutch. He came a little later on, saying that the Lord had laid Vrededorp on his heart as a field of labor. We

38

recognized that the Holy Ghost had ordained him, and now He was separating him.

We praised the Lord for what He had done, and laid our hands on the brother in token of recognition of what the Holy Ghost had done in him, and of his separation unto the ministry, and sent him forth. For the first few days miraculous healings were reported. I have personally gone with this brother, to examine many of those who were healed, and, as I have said before, have found some of the most miraculous cases of healing I have ever known – not in ones and twos, but in hundreds. On one afternoon I called on seventy people who had been healed, in the suburb where his work is.

There are only about twelve hundred people in this locality. The Plymouth Brethren Church of Vrededorp practically came into the work as a body – and ended up by baptizing every one of them. And them not as a unit, but one by one, until they are practically all in the work. The pungent, forceful transforming character of the Gospel of Jesus Christ through the power of the blood as presented compelled these brethren and sisters to say that the Lord was doing a "new thing," which was so wrought in our hearts that they wanted a part in it.

The Lord is raising up a strong band of strong Christian workers right here on the field. These new workers already speak English, and at least Dutch. Dutch is absolutely necessary for personal ministry in South

Africa. Many of these people have been so associated with the natives from their childhood that in not a few cases they speak as many as four, and sometimes six, native languages, and most everybody here can speak at least one native language.

In the people's homes they have native help (every house at least has a native kitchen-boy), and they must speak his language to him; consequently nearly every one can speak one native language; and so, the thing that is in my heart is that as missionaries equipped for the field, these people whom the Lord is raising up and baptizing with the Holy Ghost, are a better class of missionaries than the average foreign missionary.

Again, people in Africa do not live in the luxurious way that the Americans have been accustomed to. In a missionary home where I visited recently, a man who has the most pungent native work that I have ever found in Africa, (touching twenty-five thousand natives, with fifty under-preachers), tells me that he and his family live frequently six and eight months at a time on nothing but cornmeal mush and cornmeal bread. Not many American missionaries that I have run across up to this time are willing to face these things.

This man of whom I told you, Brother Mahond, does not receive a cent of support from the native people to whom he ministers. With no organization behind him to support him in any way, he is compelled to operate a farm in order to maintain himself and family.

The natives support their own local preacher by paying tithes, which they are taught to do. This man, being compelled to farm, much of his time is taken up with his farm instead of with the gospel. This ought not to be.

A man with several native languages, also Dutch and English, who in four years' time has been able to reach twenty-five thousand natives, is too valuable in the kingdom of God to be spending his time on a farm to support himself.

My thought is that there is a large mission for the American Apostolic Faith Movement other than the mere sending to individual missionaries in the field – it is the sending of their offerings and tithes.

Brother Jack Armstrong, one of our local preachers, on one occasion had a call to Rustenberg. He had no money with which to go. He came to me, and we made it a subject of prayer. The Lord finally indicated to my soul the time when he ought to go I said to him, "Brother, the Lord indicated to me that you ought to go next Wednesday."

On Wednesday morning, just before he was to leave, a lady handed me one pound in gold. This was sufficient to pay his fare to Rustenberg. He went, and in ten days eight people were saved, a number were healed, about twenty received sanctification, and eight were baptized with the Holy Ghost and spoke in tongues – all for a little less than five dollars' cost to us.

I know a city of thirty thousand people where one of the mightiest Pentecostal works in Africa can be developed, and where already the most remarkable manifestations of the Holy Ghost that I believe has occurred in this latter-day movement have taken place; but Africa is recovering from a long war that has absolutely devastated the country.

John G. Lake

NEWS FROM SOUTH AFRICA

From several letters received by Brother J. G. Lake (in Johannesburg) during the past month he gave the following quotations:

"At the Tabernacle, the service yesterday morning (Sunday) opened with a soul giving herself to God. She is a married ... of Harry Van Schele's wife. Brother _____, one of our young men workers, was baptized in the Holy Ghost yesterday afternoon. In the evening service it again opened the salvation of the wife of one of the strongest brethren, Mr. Botha: at the same time another young man (brother of one of our Dutch workers) came forward and himself to God. These conversions are clear and good.

"The Nationalists presented us with housing in Braamfontein, free of rent, for two months for our services. It was their headquarters. So we are having a special series of meetings in the district of Braamfontein, Johannesburg, taking advantage of this time. They will commence tomorrow night.

"By the way, Brother Harman this week is in Basutoland and with a large company of workers, including Brother Tom, is conducting services at one of the _____, and this week will see a settlement with the _____ or all the

43

questions necessary for the opening of the our permanent campaign there.

"I have been so jealous or ambitious for God's work that, as your funds have come into my hands this year, I have continuously used them to push the work into new areas. We don't use missionary money for farms, for buildings, or anything of that kind. If these things come into existence, it must be by the local efforts of those whom the Lord has saved in their perspective localities. My great _____ has been not to permit the money sent to be used in the older work at all, but wholly in the new fields, and this is largely the secret of the dissension that came into the work at Johannesburg, but which, bless God, passed away.

"When I got your letter with the $250, I had to get into the bathroom, out of sight, and praise God for it, for I tell you we were in an awful pinch. In a great work like this, where you have a number of workers on the field in new districts and they are relying on you to stand back of them for three or four months and you fail, it makes awful havoc. Some of those fellows are squeezed hard this time, but surely Jesus will carry us through.

"The South African election is just over. No doubt you have seen the cabled news. A great deal of racial feeling was shown by this election, especially on the part of the English. There being no large majority, will compel respect on both sides.

44

"In the Ladybrand Courant I read an account this morning of the baptismal service conducted by Brother Van de Wall and Brother Tom in the Caledon River, on the Basutoland border, last Sunday, at which time a number of Dutch people in that district were baptized. I have been pleased to note these news items in the different papers concerning our work as it demonstrates that they are no longer able to ignore this work. It now takes the place of news in this country.

"We have a strong council of competent men over our work – men who can deal with any situation. The council appointed a treasurer to take charge of the monies connected with the local work. Offerings sent to me personally from overseas, or in my care, are administered by myself, after advising with the brethren at hand, especially Brother Van de Wall.

The treasurer's books include both the monies I receive from overseas and the monies received locally for the support of the general work here, and they are open to inspection at any time. For five months we received an average of $500 a month; after five months it dropped to one-half, and this month there has only been a pittance.

"Our council consists of Rev. Thomas Hezmalhalch, president: John G. Lake, vice president: Rev. R. H. Van de Wall, secretary: Rev. P. E. Le Roux. Rev. Modred Powell, J. H. Greef and Josephus Le Roux. Van de Wall was a preacher in the Dutch Reformed Church, and a

45

professor in some of their institutions: he had also practiced law; he is a strong, educated man, a teacher by profession. P. E. Le Roux was also a teacher and a preacher in the Dutch Reformed Church formerly. Greeff is a strong, godly man, as also Josephus Le Roux (who is not related to P. E. Le Roux).

"There is one thing we need here. It is the same thing that you need there – more of the mighty power of God. Can I give you an example through an incident of the week? There is a body of men in Johannesburg who call themselves Apostles and who have a body of followers. They are a sort of Mormon offshoot, I believe. They came in force to the Tabernacle Wednesday night, about thirty strong. As the service progressed it was apparently their desire to challenge the Spirit in our meeting, and according to their code of apostleship, they were supposed to have the authority to bind the Spirit.

In fact, their leader had written me a strong challenge to permit him to come to the Tabernacle and bind the Spirit. I asked one of them in the meeting, "Are you the man who wrote that letter?" He said, "Yes." I replied, "All right, brother, you get up and bind the spirit now." He proceeded with due formality to bind the Spirit. I stood quietly on the platform while this was going on, inwardly praying that when he was done, God would manifest Himself.

As he ceased speaking, I felt the Spirit fall on me, and instantly I commenced to speak in tongues. Then in a moment this occurred a second time, when, like a wave, apparently every baptized person in the house broke into tongues in rebuke in the Spirit. In an instant there was one of the most striking manifestations that I have ever known in my entire career."

Then, in closing his last letter, Brother Lake says: "Dear Brothers Studd and Fisher: Just a word before the mail closes. Do not let these things (the letters and accusations against him which have been sent from Africa) trouble you, and don't worry for us at this end of the battlefield. The work is clear, good and progressive. My soul is strong, my body is strong, and my mind clear: and the devil is on the run.

Whatever strife has been stirred up against us has been concentrated in Johannesburg. We have been having conversions, healings and baptisms in the Spirit steadily ever since I have returned from the field. I have never been more blessed or more used of God on any mission trip in my life than the long mission this summer.

"I know how letters sound on the other side of the world, but what do these things count for here, after a meeting like last night's (Sunday), when people were saved and others instantly healed of cancer, rheumatic cripples, etc., right in the presence of five hundred people? I am only sorry for the awful privations some of our workers are enduring because of offerings being largely cut off from the homeland, because of these false accusations.

But this work is going on, regardless of all that hell can do. It is God's work, and men cannot stop it. The work throughout the country never moved more blessedly than in the last six months. Our native work is strong, good and clear: and it is being extended with marvelous rapidity."

Good-by. God bless you all.

John G. Lake

A CALL FOR HELPERS

Johannesburg, Transvaal

Dear Sister Smock:

I want to make this letter strictly business. I know your soul is wrapped up in missionary work; so is mine. I want you to realize in some degree what I can only tell you that Johannesburg is unquestionably the greatest field for missionary work in the known world. In the last three or four years the natives from the very interior of Africa have been coming up to Johannesburg to work on the mines. They live on the compounds and on any Sunday forenoon YOU CAN ADDRESS 2500 NATIVES in most of the compounds.

About 150 mines are in operation each of which employs from 1,000 to 3,000 natives who are accommodated in compounds, buildings built in a square with a court in the center, where an additional building is placed as a kitchen. These compounds are scattered along the railroad at the various mines for fifty miles.

The thing that my heart is on is this, that some of these souls who have been waiting and preparing and praying and praying, and apparently getting nowhere, get into

God's order of getting things from Him and come as God has called them, and commence to use the faith they have got, and as they use it they will get more.

Oh, beloved, God is doing a wonderful work here. I cannot tell you what wonderful manifestations of the Spirit of God that we see every day, in depth of character a hundred times beyond anything I have ever seen anywhere. But there is such a demand for workers at this time. I could place a hundred workers today if they were only here.

Sister Smock, in Jesus' name, do get a hold on some of the home people and get them into clearer light and real faith in God and believe Him for coming here.

There are FIFTY THOUSAND CHINESE HERE. They live in compounds too. The Chinese Missionary from Canton who ministers to them was baptized with the Holy Ghost at one of our cottage meetings a week ago last night. He is a precious fellow. One of the Baker missionaries, Bro. Ingram, has received his baptism. A Dutch Missionary next door to where we live, Mr. Van Marile, has received his baptism.

The Congregational Church at Pretoria, after observing the healings there, have commenced to pray for the sick, and one young man in the last stages of consumption was healed in answer to their prayers. One of the Baker missions has commenced to pray for the sick. Two sick natives were brought to their meetings and were instantly healed and praised God in a wonderful way.

I do have it in my soul that GOD WANTS TO USE YOU in America as a recruiting officer and to take up some of these people who have calls and get them out here.

These people that are wondering about where they are called to, if they have got a call anywhere, God can use them here. There are not only hundreds of thousands of natives, and Chinamen, but there are thousands of Mohammedans and natives of India all over Africa. If they have got a call to India, this is India enough. If they have a call to China, this is China enough. But dear Sister Smock, one thing that I can be assured of, you will not encourage anyone of doubtful or insincere experience to come.

Your Brother In Christ,

John G. Lake

"The Upper Room" Letters
August 1909

Written: June 7th, 1909, South Africa

"I have been absent for some time amongst the Zulus at Wakkerstrom on the Transvaal and Natal borders. We had a very remarkable meeting there; it commenced on Saturday night and lasted until 12 o'clock on Monday. The natives never even stopped to eat. Sixteen were baptized with the Holy Ghost that we know of, and no doubt there were many others whom we did not know.

The power of God came down upon the gathering at 2:30 on Sunday afternoon in a wonderful way, and for several hours afterwards people were getting the baptism in all sections of the building. Fully a hundred could not get into the building, so we went outside and held an open air service with them, and three received the baptism outside. At every service while we were there, baptisms occurred, and I feel it is the beginning of a mighty stir amongst the Zulus in that district.

"Our Elder there, Brother Le Roux, is an Africander (i.e. a European born in Africa): he is a Boer, and of course speaks Dutch; he also speaks Zulu, and I think Basuto. He is an earnest man of God, ministering to about ten thousand people, through twenty-five local preachers

53

and three evangelists who assist him – all natives. The Lord has baptized several of these preachers, and the rest are earnestly seeking their Pentecost.

"At a baptismal service held by Brother Le Roux some weeks ago the following remarkable incident occurred: after the third candidate had come up out of the water, and as the fourth was being baptized, the Spirit fell on the meeting there in the open air, and that fourth man came out of the water speaking in tongues. And after that the Holy Spirit fell upon every single one as they were being baptized, and they all came up out of the water baptized with the Holy Ghost and speaking in tongues.

I called upon Brother Schwede yesterday: he is improving slowly though he is still confined to his bed. He is in splendid hands, stopping in the home of Brother and Sister VandeBile in one of the suburbs of Johannesburg. You can hardly realize how near he came to going home. One of the native ministers who knew Schwede, Brother Letwaba, while praying for him, had a vision of him lying on a cot and an angel standing at the head of the bed: and on a white banner was this scripture, Psalm 118:17, 18. 'I shall not die but live, and declare the works of our Lord. The Lord hath chastened me more, but he has not given me unto death.' We received his letter on Saturday night when Schwede was at the very lowest; and in the middle of the night when many of us were praying, the Spirit of the Lord came upon one of us, Mrs. Dockrell, and she arose under the power of the Spirit and went from the parlor into Schwede's room and kneeling by his bedside prayed. While she prayed the Spirit fell upon Schwede and that dying man began to plead for his life as I never heard any one plead for life. God heard and a marked change in his condition took place and he has been recovering ever since. I should not be surprised if he is in harness again very soon although we generally find that it takes some time for people to build up after a severe attack of this African fever, which is especially deadly this year.

The work throughout the country is progressing well, and it is specially encouraging in the country districts. Our congregation here is settling down to a normal basis; the tabernacle last night was filled, both sitting and standing room. Give my love to all the dear saints with you. Be assured that we do appreciate your loving sympathy and your prayers, as well as your financial assistance. You brother in Christ.

John G. Lake.

THE POSITION
OF THE
APOSTOLIC FAITH

MISSION OF SOUTH AFRICA

On the subject of the Sabbath as given by the President, Rev. John G. Lake, October 6, 1912, at the Annual Conference:

During the Conference I was asked by the brethren to deliver a discourse on the subject of the Sabbath Day for the guidance of the workers. It is not my purpose to deal with the subject in an argumentative manner, but rather in the form of a pronouncement of the position of the Apostolic Faith Mission of South Africa on the question.

The Word of God is sufficiently clear. It has already defined the position for the Christian in the most emphatic way. The 2nd chapter of Colossians is perhaps as clear a portion of Scripture on this particular issue as any portion of the Word. It seems most difficult indeed for Christians to understand and realize, in our entrance into Christ Jesus by the reception of the Spirit of God who abides within, our Christian experience has been moved into a different place from that in which we lived before.

I have tried at different times to define the operation of the Spirit of God in the different dispensations, that we may get a clear basis on which to rest. I will review this this morning in a word.

THE PATRIARCHAL DISPENSATION

In the Patriarchal dispensation God seems to have been approaching man from this standpoint, as if man was far removed from God, and as if God was endeavoring to reveal Himself to man. Abraham perhaps furnishes the best example in the Word, and to him God appeared twice, twenty years apart. There was a lapse of twenty years, in which Abraham heard nothing from God. Then God spoke to him again. Now, that is the best revelation from God to man that is given us in the Patriarchal dispensation. And it seems as if the position was, "God revealing Himself to man."

THE MOSAIC DISPENSATION

The Mosaic Dispensation was different. It was a fueled revelation. It did not destroy any of the revelation of God that the Patriarchs had known. It developed and expanded their revelation. So God was present with the Jewish people in the Pillar of Cloud and the Pillar of

58

Fire, and the Shekinah over the Mercy Seat, an ever present God.

When the Temple was built, the Lord abode in the Holy of Holies. In it there was no artificial light. The Outer Court was lit by twelve candles, but in the Holy of Holies there was neither window or door, no artificial light of any kind. The presence of God illuminated the Holy of Holies, the continuous abiding presence of God with man.

THE CHRISTIAN DISPENSATION

Patriarchal revelation was "God to man," and the Mosaic revelation was "God with man;" but the Christian revelation is greater than all, for Jesus said in His own words, "He dwelleth with you, and shall be IN you." And the revelation of God to the Christian is "Christ within you" by the Holy Ghost, not "to" man, nor "with" man, but "in" man. Man becoming the embodiment of God.

It will be readily seen, then, that our conception and standard must be in accordance with the revelation that God gave to us, and the Christian cannot base his standard of life upon the Mosaic Law in any way. Jesus lifted us above that standard; as high as the heavens are above the earth.

When the Christian, then, endeavors to go back and live under Christ Jesus and the communion of the control of the law, he has descended from the standard of the Spirit of God abiding within, and has placed himself in the same position where the Mosaic people were.

PAUL'S WARNINGS

Over and over again Paul warns us about this thing, and to the Galatians particularly he gives that wonderful warning that having begun in the Spirit they were now going to return to the flesh. And that is the danger with many Christians these days, that having begun in the Holy Ghost, they might return to obedience to Commandments.

THE LORD JESUS RAISES THE STANDARD FOR THE CHRISTIAN DISPENSATION

Then someone says: "What about the Commandments!" We can see what Jesus says of them in the Sermon on the Mount. Matt 5:21, Jesus said, "It was said by them of old time, Thou shalt not kill." But Jesus lifted that standard miles above where Moses placed it and said, "But I say unto you, That whosoever is angry with his brother without a cause is in danger of the judgment." That is to say, he is a murderer. 1 John 3:15

Under the Mosaic Law they had to commit an act in order to be guilty. Under the law of Christ the presence in the heart of the desire is sufficient to condemn. So in every instance the Lord raised the standard.

The Commandment says, "Thou shalt not commit adultery," but Jesus says, "That whosoever looketh on a woman to lust after her hath committed adultery with her already in his heart." Jesus takes it out of the regime of Commandment into the regime of the heart experience, and "as the heavens are higher than the earth, so are My ways higher than your ways and My thoughts than your thoughts." Isaiah 55:9

THE GREAT DEBATE

The great debate that has come through these fifty years, between those who contend for the observance of the Sabbath Day (the Seventh) and we who accept the Christian Sabbath, has ever been on that one point. Are we still bound by the law or has Christ made the Christian free from the force of the Commandment? And it seems to me that the Word of God makes this clear as daylight, that the Word places our feet emphatically on this ground that to us, in the Holy Ghost, the law has become a dead thing.

Indeed, it has been spoken of as blotted out (Col. 2:14), even that which was written on stone (2 Cor. 3:7), taken

61

out of the regime of Commandment, burned in the conscience and stamped upon the soul. Blessed be God!

The first chapter of Colossians deals with the history of the indwelling of Christ, and after this fact of the indwelling is clearly established, Paul goes on to review the subject of our obedience to Christ and the law.

Commencing with the 13th verse of the 2nd chapter, we have the declaration of the expulsion of the law: "And you, being dead in your sins and the un-circumcision of your flesh, hath He quickened together with Him, having forgiven you all trespasses blotting out the handwriting of ordinances that was against us, which was contrary to us, and took it out of the way, nailing it to His cross; and having spoiled principalities and powers, He made a shew of them openly, triumphing over them in it. Let no man therefore judge you in meat, or in drink, or in respect of an holy day, or of the new moon, or of the Sabbath Days; which are a shadow of things to come; but the body is of Christ."

Thus far the interpretation is given of the destruction by Christ of the ordinances and laws that were contrary to us by having established within us by the Holy Ghost, the fact of His own indwelling, He having been the Lord of the Sabbath, and we, as sons of God and joint heirs with Jesus Christ, will also enter into that place of dominion, where we, too, in Him, have become lords

also of the Sabbath and every other commandment.
Blessed be God!

THE NEW COVENANT

The 16th verse: On Thursday last, among the questions
that were asked, was this: "Do we advocate the
partaking of a meal in connection with the Lord's
Supper!" And in this things once again we see the
Christian's failure to separate between the Old and the
New Dispensations.

For, when Jesus partook officially of the last Passover
Supper that was ever given to mankind and by that act
forever closed the Jewish Dispensation, there was
nothing further to do but make the sacrifice on the
Cross, and the instant after the closing of that Supper the
Lord instituted a new ceremony, the one we observe
today, the Communion of the Lord's Supper. No longer
the Passover feast and Passover lamb, but the Christ of
God, Who now pledges Himself to shed His own blood
for the salvation of the world.

Between these two acts there is as great a distance as
between East and West. The one was the mark and
stamp of that which was old and ready to decay (Heb.
8:13), and the other was the birth of mankind through
the shedding of the blood of Jesus Christ. And so,
beloved, when the Christian undertakes that his life shall

63

be governed by Commandments, he is going back again into this old life, into the old realm, forgetting his state with Christ Jesus.

It does not mean that we shall turn anarchists and that to us there is no law, but rather that we are now obedient unto the higher law, by the Son of God.

THE SABBATH DAY

On the subject of the Sabbath itself: All the other Commandments are spoken of in the New Testament and reiterated, but the Sabbath Commandment, isn't; and that no doubt, for this reason, that the prophecies all along had pointed to the Son of God, who was Himself the fulfillment of the law. "I came not to destroy the law, but to fulfill it." (Matt. 5:17) "For the law was our schoolmaster to bring us unto Christ." When we got to Christ, beloved, we were beyond the sphere of the law. The law was a schoolmaster to bring us to Christ. Blessed be His name! (Gal.3:24)

So with the Sabbath. Christ Himself, the Eternal Rest into which the Christian enters, not to abide on the Sabbath Day, but to abide always, every day, and forever; He is our Sabbath alone.

When we live in the Son of God we have come beyond the sphere of commandment, for the law was made for

64

the unlawful and unholy, for murderers of fathers and mothers, for whoremongers, etc. (1 Timothy 1:9, 10). Upon our statute books today there are no doubt a thousand laws that you and I know nothing about, and we care less. Why? They are of no interest to us. We hardly pay any attention to the law of murder, nor can we tell the details because of the fact that being sons of God we are living in love and are not interested in what the law says of murder. There is no murder in our hearts. Blessed be God! We have passed on.

And so the Christian who enters into Christ Jesus and is abiding in Him and is a possessor of the Holy Ghost, has moved beyond the regime of the law and commandments. They are of no value to him. He lives in obedience to one law and one commandment, the Eleventh. That includes all the rest in one: "That ye love one another as I have loved you." (John 15:12) Blessed be His name.

AN APT ILLUSTRATION

Henry Drummond, I believe it is, in his "Greatest Thing in the World," gives an illustration that is so fitting. He says that he visits at a friend's home. He finds that he and his wife have lived together in the most beautiful unity for many years. But a friend of his is still anxious that he shall be a strict observer of the law, and he sits down and writes a code of the rules for the government

65

of this man and wife who have always lived together in unity. He says, "Thou shalt not kill her. Thou shalt not bear false witness against her. Thou shalt not steal from her," and so on through the other commandments. He takes it up and laughs. Of what value is such a code to him? Has he not for all the years past been giving to his wife his heart's affection that makes it impossible for such things to enter his soul? And there is just that much difference between the Christian standard and the standard of the law.

May God help us that we shall not take backward steps, but realize our position as sons of God. We shall live in Him and abide in the Holy Ghost and realize the freedom of sons, not the bondage of servants. Blessed be His name. Nevertheless, to the man outside of Christ the commandment still stands. As on our statute books today the law of murder applies to the man who commits murder, but the man in Christ has passed beyond that sphere. "Let no man therefore judge you in meat, or drink, or in respect of an holy day, or of the new moon, or of the Sabbath days; which are a shadow of things to come; but the body is of Christ. Blessed be His name! Blessed be His name!

OUR HIGH CHRISTIAN PRIVILEGE

Now, will we never get the force of the 2nd Chapter of Colossians where the Word portrays the exaltation of the

Son of God, even to the sitting down at the right hand of the Father in the Heavenly places far above all principality, and power and might, and dominion, and every name that is named. (Eph. 1:19-23) And the second chapter of Ephesians portraying our lifting up out of the regime of death and sin, into the same exaltation of the Son of God, until we realize our high privileges in Christ Jesus.

Indeed. I have this in my heart that the low state of Christian experience that is common among men, is mostly accounted for by this one fact, that Christians have failed to grasp the exalted place into which Jesus Christ puts us when we have been made sons of God. May God write that deep in our soul, that we may keep not the Seventh Day (which was a shadow of things to come, but THE BODY IS OF CHRIST), not the commandments, but by holy Christian privilege one day sacred to God, and that without any commandment at all, but out of the gladness of the Christian heart.

Blessed be His name, one day is set aside in commemoration of his resurrection, but with the Christian, and in the life in Christ Jesus, every day is as holy as every other, and there is no distinction of days whatever, for the life is in Him (in the Son of God), and He is the same every day. Blessed be His name.

THE FIRST DAY

But, beloved, have not we cause to rejoice that in Christianity there has been established a day of commemoration of His resurrection, and that altogether the Christian world unite in exalting the Son of God by keeping that day holy. We may not let down on our reverence for the First Day of the week; but may we as Christians exalt the day not by obedience to commandment, but, as Jesus Himself did, by making it a day when His life was given forth for the benefit of others, and I know God will bless us.

Now, I hope that forever this question is settled in our hearts. That, so far as the Apostolic Faith Mission is concerned, we stand in Christ Jesus in the union of the Holy Ghost; and do you know that Thursday afternoon was one of the most important days that ever occurred in this Mission, for on that day, God, by the unity of His Spirit helped this Conference to come together and to recognize the fact that every man has the privilege to be led by the Spirit, not to observe all the law, but led by His Spirit.

"THE UPPER ROOM" LETTERS
NOVEMBER 1910

THE POWER OF HEALING

As an illustration of the mighty power of healing as a part of the Gospel and an entering wedge for it, we quote the following account of a cottage meeting held recently in a suburb of Johannesburg, South Africa:

"On Tuesday night, at a cottage meeting in Braanfontein, Johannesburg, at the home of Brother and Sister Philles, as the meeting progressed, the Lord was baptizing some in the Spirit, and while others were praying I commenced to observe who the people present were, and was struck to note that almost everyone in the room was a miracle of God in salvation or healing.

"The first was Brother Philles himself, who had been a drunkard of the worst type. His dear wife, with the glory of God shining on her face, had been healed of a great internal tumor, and is rejoicing in the Lord with her husband.

Brother Kotze, whose wife, two weeks ago Sunday, was dying, and from three in the afternoon until ten at night was unconscious, and practically dead. She tells of her experience as being on the other side, and of what transpired during this time. The onlookers say she was to all intents practically dead. In answer to the prayer of Brother and Sister Van de Wall, she was instantly healed, and in ten minutes sat up in bed and ate Boer bread and drank coffee."

"Next to them sat Brother Hanger, a former city detective, who had been blind and paralyzed. There is still the effect of paralysis (a trace of it) about the brother, but God gave him his sight instantly, and nine-tenths of his healing of paralysis. His daughter was baptized in the Holy Ghost at this meeting to which I refer. His dear wife, who also had been saved and healed, sat by his side.

"Next to them were Brother and Sister Schultz, who have both been saved and sanctified, and Brother Schults baptized in the Holy Ghost. Sister Schultz was healed when in a dying state, during our absence in America. Their little son Louis, had quick consumption, and curvature of the spine, so that his spine was like the letter "S" and his one shoulder inches above the other on account of the curve in the spine. He had been given up to die by four physicians, who assured the parents that there was no hope for him. He was healed, and is now entirely well. Their baby was healed when dying.

"Mrs. Arlow, healed of internal cancer called varicose veins, a very common disease in Africa, affecting both men and women. Who testifies that the ulcers on the veins were an inch in diameter. That while she saw the Tabernacle, being a sinner, a Magdal — she did not feel worthy to ask us to pray for her, but as we prayed for others her own heart cry went up to God, and God instantly healed her of both diseases. She said a warm wind passed over her body, and to her amazement, when she arose to go home, she felt herself well. Her husband who was a great drunkard, came to Tabernacle, we cast the devils out of a man and he had been saved and sanctified.

"Next to them was little Norah Richards, a girl of about twelve years of age, who instantly healed of a totally deaf ear, with her other ear being partly deaf. She was baptized in the Holy Ghost at the service.

"An old man, eighty-three years old, while in a meeting, about a month ago, told by the Spirit of God to be baptized in water. He obeyed God. His son, a young man, has been baptized in the Holy Ghost and is speaking in tongues.

"Brother Kemp, formerly a deacon in the Dutch Church, now baptized in the Holy Ghost, is mightily used of God in getting others saved and healed.

"Sister May, saved, sanctified and baptized in the Holy Ghost, was healed very bad case of rheumatism.

"Brother Herholdt, saved and sanctified and healed of rheumatism and indigestion of long standing.

"Brother Rollinson, saved and sanctified and baptized in the Holy Ghost. Her brother's arm was broken recently through being run over by a cart. The Lord healed the man's arm.

"Mrs. Smith, saved, and healed of varicose veins.

Mrs. Alexander, healed of tuberculosis of the bone in her arm, after two unsuccessful operations. She is baptized in the Holy Ghost. Next to her was her _____ Mrs. Hunt, sanctified and baptized in the Holy Ghost recently. Her husband was saved two weeks after her baptism.

Now, if you will go down this list of single cottage meeting, you will see how the power of healing in this Gospel has been in Africa.

John G. Lake

"THE UPPER ROOM" LETTERS OCTOBER 1910

LETTER OF CONFIDENCE

P.O. Box 1420, Johannesburg, Oct. 3, 1910

Messengers G. B. Studd and E. K. Fisher.

Dear Brothers in Christ:

In view of the fact that the most infamous lies and vilest slander is being circulated against the work and certain workers of the Apostolic Faith Mission, particularly Brother Lake, and as we deeply appreciate the full Gospel of Christ Jesus preached by him and his earnest and devoted service for the advancement of the Kingdom of Christ, and as we have the best interests of the work and its progression at heart, we feel it our bounden duty to take some action whereby we express our utter disgust and disapproval of such malignancy and procedures of so degrading a character, which manifestly are the outcome of jealous and petty minds.

At the same time our hearts rejoice and overflow with gratefulness to our Mighty God and Savior for saving, sanctifying, healing, baptizing in His Holy Spirit, and blessing hundreds of souls through the ministry of

73

Brother Lake. Where once all was darkness and sorrow, now the Light of Jesus shines, and peace reigns. Hundreds of homes have been the happier and purer and more Christlike for his influence. To prove these statements we purpose making a collection of personally signed testimonies which will be submitted to you as soon as possible. It will be apparent from these how mightily the man has been used of God: it may also give you a revelation of the magnitude of the work. His ministry extends over a vast space of country, entailing much expense (as absolute necessities are costly here).

But endued with a constant burning zeal for the glory of his Master, he has pushed on in spite of the mountains of difficulty and adversity that comes, sacrificing all comfort and often going without the necessaries of life to accomplish something for his Savior. The Spirit of the Living God is so manifest in his life that through all he has shown a sweet spirit of humility that has won the hearts of many: though the fiery darts of the Evil One have fallen thick around him, he has stood firm in the spirit of forgiveness and held a still tongue.

We do not write thus to eulogize man that he may take to himself glory; no, but in true humbleness of heart we do it that the mighty works of the Lord may be made known, and the Name of the Lord of Hosts magnified. We feel that the time has come when the faithful should rally together as true brothers and sisters in Christ and let the true state of affairs be made known.

It is sad indeed to see how Satan has crept in and used those who were apparently on the Lord's side to mar God's wonderful work. May a merciful God bring them to repentance and forgive.

We praise God for the blessed privileges of living in South Africa and being partakers of such a marvelously wonderful salvation. Some say the days of miracles are past, Hallelujah! We can shout no! The same God that delivered and blessed Elijah and Daniel lives today. Souls are saved, the blind see, the lame walk, the brokenhearted receive comfort, those bound by vice and sin are set free, the bruised are liberated, the blessed Gospel of the Light of Jesus Christ is preached to the poor, faith in Christ's redeeming work is strengthened, and hearts are revitalized with a passion for the saving of souls. Surely this is the will of the Father.

We beseech you earnestly to join with us in presenting our petitions before the Throne of Grace, that the power of Satan may be broken, that nothing may hinder the work of the Lord, that the urgent needs of the work and workers may be supplied, that all may be united in a bond of love, that they may keep the unity of the Spirit in the bond of peace, for we are one body in Christ, and every one members of one another.

As it has come to our notice that you have received letter condemning Brother Lake and his teachings, we beg of you to hold over your judgment until you see the personal testimonies of many in this land. It might be well to mention that not one of the recognized workers have had anything to do with the writings of this letter we the undersigned being simply Christian members of the congregation prompted by the burning desire that the Truth should prevail, and God's work continue in peace and purity.

In conclusion we would like to take this opportunity of expressing our appreciation of the good work that is being done and the fine spirit of endurance that is being shown by the younger workers in the field. They are faithfully bearing the burden and heat of the day without murmur; in some instances they have existed on the most lowly fare, and have had nothing but the canopy of heaven to shelter them at night. Pray much for the work in Africa.

We greet you all in the Name of Jesus, may He abundantly bless your work in America. We are

Your brothers and Sisters in Christ.

Georgy Ulyate   Mrs. B. Dakrall.

J. Albert Lind.   Jacob Gouws.

M. Lind.   J. Bethel Etc., Etc

The above letter, written spontaneously speaks for itself. We have many other personal letters of testimony from different ones in South Africa who have been saved, healed and blessed through the ministry of our dear Brother John G. Lake – (Ed.)

In Johannesburg

Of the work in Johannesburg Brother Lake writes:

"God has been doing a blessed work here in Johannesburg right along, and we have been getting in a number of better and stronger people than have come into our work for some time. One dear brother, Welch, who received the baptism of the Holy Ghost last Monday, gives promise of being a most devout soul and strong worker. Another, Brother Sharp, who was saved at our open-air meeting about three months ago, is a fine strong character, and is developing into a splendid worker; also Brother Heatley and his wife.

"Brother Heatley has had the most wonderful healing of a diseased bone in the head, which had been treated at a great hospital in England for years. He also had a paralyzed hand, caused by the tendons being cut in a machinery accident, which refused to heal, though he was nine months in hospital. Of all this God healed him! Now he has been baptized with the Holy Ghost for some months, and is a most precious, strong worker. He takes charge of our open-air meetings in the market square, and much other work besides.

"Last Wednesday we had rather a quiet meeting, and after the meeting the people were standing around and greeting each other. I just felt hungry for something doing, and so I went around to some and asked them to come into the little vestry if they wanted to. A few came. There is a Mr. Sharp here. He told me on Wednesday that he had been saved six weeks. We went to the market square one Saturday night for an open-air meeting, and took with us, on a cart, our Tabernacle piano and organ. This Mr. Sharp said that in spite of himself, he could not resist following. He was drunk, and his friends tried to keep him away, but invariably he found himself fastened by something he could not control, and held to that open-air meeting. The result was that he was saved unto God, fully saved.

He has been busy ever since. Sunday morning he faithfully goes to Brakpan by train, and conducts native meetings. His wife is at present visiting in England, and he is earnestly praying for her salvation. A week ago Sunday, his young son, about seventeen, I think, was beautifully converted. You ought to see how earnestly he is also praying for his baptism for, like his father, he is very hungry for it, and God has favored him by putting His precious power on him.

"After the meeting on Wednesday we just stayed with Brother Sharp until the Lord baptized him. I do not know how late, but I stayed, also, and you ought to have heard it bubble out of him in mighty power, like a windmill. Isn't it wonderful, His coming into our very bodies?

80

Verily, it is true, what the poet says:

> 'Speak to Him, thou for He hears,
>
> and Spirit with spirit can meet:
>
> Closer is He than breathing,
>
> And nearer than hands and feet.'

"It is so sweet to watch the enthusiasm with which these dear ones are pressing on when the enemy is trying to overthrow this work. Pray for some of God's little ones who are shaky through this work of the enemy in our midst.

"The atmosphere was so clear in the Spirit on Sunday morning as it has not been for a long time. The people were impelled to get up and praise God, breaking into the meeting continually in order to get their testimony in.

"One brother writes from New Zealand that at the time we prayed for him he had chronic asthma and catarrh. He was healed. This occurred before the handkerchief which they had sent returned to him.

"Thursday we went to pray for a woman forty miles away, who has a bleeding cancer in her womb, and the Lord touched her, but it is not yet a complete healing. Please pray for perfect healing for her.

"Mr. H. asked for prayer for a man in the hospital who was dying: I think it was with appendicitis. Nine doctors had tried to help, but said nothing could be done for him. We prayed at the Tabernacle, and yesterday, after three weeks, Mr. S. went there again, and found the man sitting up. The doctors say it is a miracle, and give him all kinds of concessions. It is so wonderful to them. They call him 'The Resurrection.' Very appropriate, isn't it? Our God answers prayer, and has not lost His power. Praise His name!

"On Thursday last we were told of one of our dear members who was dying. He was there on Sunday morning, and gave his testimony—how he was told that he was growing cold, but he said he felt hot, and he prayed with earnestness after the saints had left him, and God raised him up. You ought to have seen the astonishment with which the dear saints who knew of his condition looked at him. Oh, hallelujah! What a wonderful salvation from a wonderful Savior!

"Several who have been fighting us have died and been buried, others are very ill, and one reported insane. We are living in awful times. It looks very much like the sin against the Holy Ghost, doesn't it?

God is so anxious to do something these days, and He has only us poor, weak, unwise mortals to do it with, that He will have His way, and everyone who gets in the way suffers. Oh, I want to be so yielded that, no matter what I have to suffer, and what it costs, He may work His workings through me."

GOD IS STILL
WORKING MIGHTILY

SOUTH AFRICA

From Brother Lake's most recent letters, written towards the {illegible}, we give some quotations, which show how blessedly God is working in the South African field, especially amongst the Dutch and the natives. There have been some most striking answers to prayer in the way that money has come at critical moments, showing very plainly that at the back of this work is the Lord Himself. It is small wonder to us that the devil should stir up all the opposition he can and use every instrument, human or otherwise, to hinder the mighty work which God is doing.

It has commonly been true, too, that God has chosen leaders who have rarely been understood by their own generation. The more {illegible} conspicuously God puts a man to the front of this warfare, the more surely may he expect to meet fierce opposition, and to have to stand very much alone. It's also true that prominent leaders whom God is using need very specially the prayers of the saints everywhere that they may have courage and faith sufficient to be used of God.

85

Also grace enough to keep them humble and unselfish when He does so use them. So let us pray specially at this time for Brother John G. Lake. He is bearing big burdens in the work and God is using him mightily.

Writing form Kopje (Orange River Colony) May 21, he says:

"Brother Vandewall and I arrived here in this Boer farming district from Johannesburg. Last night we held a meeting at Brother Van Scale's, a blessed man of God. Forty have been baptized by Christian baptism and a large number in the Holy Ghost.

"Oh, how I wish you might be here to see God moving among this people. Men are hungry in this sparsely settled country, and instead of one here and there accepting salvation, here it seems that whole districts come together and yield to God. It is very similar to the work of the early Methodists in America.

"The Boers are a slow-moving, deep thinking people. You can win them for God if you take time, but you must move with care and patience. My familiarity with the traditions and history of the Huguenots has been of good service, and I am now reading up the history of the early Dutch in South Africa. The Boers intensely love the traditions of their race. In our meeting last night, God led me out on the line of the life and character of the Huguenots, who were the early founders of South Africa.

Later, they were intermarried and absorbed by the Dutch. I showed them that the Huguenots came to Africa for Jesus' sake, and to escape the persecutions of the Catholic power after the Edict of Nantes. They came in the power of God and many were baptized in the Holy Ghost: they spake in tongues like ourselves, prophesied in the Spirit, and were known in France as "The Tremblers" because they shook under the power of God. The sick were healed, as with us, in fact the Boer people were their children, and the spirit of faith that possessed these early settlers is not dead.

It is latent, and the touch of God through the Holy Ghost is causing the old faith flame to burn, and the spirit and power have been manifested today. As I spoke the latent fire in a school teacher's soul made him arise and address the meeting, and God mightily used his words to convince the audience indeed. God is moving very mightily among the Boers this year, and many new workers are rising up from their ranks.

"May 22nd. Since writing the above, we have had three meetings at different centers. Last night the Spirit fell in a wonderful way, prostrating many of the congregation and baptizing several. This morning at our 'white' service, God by the Holy Ghost separated eight new Boer workers to their ministry. I tell you, brethren, it is

87

good to see God making missionaries eight at a time, all well-developed strong men, full of God and Holy Ghost fire.

This morning the Spirit seemed to come in waves over the audience, and the power and glory was such that we could do nothing but praise, not preach. It was glorious. Brother Vandewall had never seen the power fall like that. Last night in the middle of the meeting a native came forward with inflammation of the lungs, and a bad shoulder, the result of a broken collar-bone. Jesus instantly healed him, and he went away rejoicing. Then a white brother with stomach and liver disease was healed like a flash of lightning: and as we laid hands on the workers who were going forth, the power fell so that we could hardly pray in the past two months. God has raised up fifteen new Dutch workers, and they almost all support themselves.

They own their farms, and spend their time in the Gospel. Truly it is wonderful how the Holy Ghost is moving. Almost everyone in this locality has been saved, and are one with us in this Gospel. In preaching to the natives, the Lord makes me preach continually from "Ye must be born again."

Johannesburg, May 24th: "I arrived home last night. You will rejoice with me that Brother Van Schele is again going out into the work, and God's power is upon him. He was one of those, who had gone into business in order to support his family just before we returned from America. Now God is putting both him and Kretzschmar back into the work. Brethren, truly, a wonderful anointing from heaven has commenced to fall on this work again, let your beloved saints know that God has answered prayer, but in their rejoicing do not let them forget to pray continually.

"A movement has commenced amongst the Dutch people like this in several different localities, they have rented or bought a farm as a center and home for workers who are out on the field to come back to for rest. These will also make centers in the various localities around which the work will concentrate. It is God who is moving, not man, nor men. My time is now largely occupied in arranging and ordering the work, rather than in personal ministry, yet I never give up entirely the personal ministry. I used to be called upon to come and preach; now on my table today lay calls from six different localities separated by hundreds of miles, asking me to put the body in order. The Lord has already saved the people, and brought them together.

"I will give you a few incidents to show how wonderfully God is working: A man named Vereere, an influential farmer, whose wife was very much interested in this work, and was seeking her baptism (she was also an invalid, and needed healing), he was very much against this work, but in a dream the Lord appeared to him and told him that in two days, two brethren would come as representatives of this work and that he was to receive them and that through them his whole house would be blessed.

"On Saturday night my brother and Van Schele slept on the prairie, or veldt, not far from this house, having had no place to go the night before. In the morning at daylight, they saw this house, and as they approached it, the brother met them in the yard, invited them to come into the house and have breakfast and conduct worship with the family, which they did.

The power of God came down upon the household in a wonderful way. The man himself was saved. His wife was healed, and another young man in the home was saved. In fact the whole household was saved. Then they got anxious about their son-in-law and married daughter who live on another farm not very far away, and they all set to praying for them. In the course of a day they were attending a meeting at one of the brother's home, for in Africa we have meetings in the daytime and in the nighttime both.

We send word to the country announcing a meeting at a certain time, and the people come even if it is a workday and, if necessary, they will stay two or three days while God works. This young man and his wife came to this meeting and were both saved. In three days a number of families in the neighborhood were saved, and God has started a wonderful work.

Then they felt they should go to Basutoland: though they knew no one there and had never been in Basutoland before. They were about 20 miles from the boundary. They rode on their bicycles. The day before they arrived the mother of a native chief had a remarkable dream in which the Lord told her that the next day at 12 o'clock some white men would come of a different religion from theirs, and that they were to receive them in the name of the Lord and that through them the people would be greatly blessed. She went around all over the Kraal and told the people in the morning what the Lord had shown her. Her son was the chief and she also told him. The mother herself had a great internal tumor.

"At 12 o'clock precisely, the brethren came, as the Lord had saith, and when they came they found the whole Kraal in excitement of expectation awaiting them. The woman was healed. The chief gave his heart to God. The old mother herself was converted and Brother Van Schele told me this morning that so far as he was able to know the entire Kraal was saved.

"The Lord is moving mightily among the Dutch people in Africa at this time. The general conditions in the work are largely like they were when the great anointing of God was upon this work a year and a half ago. Marvelous things are happening every day. For example, where I was ministering, having just returned from Cape Colony a young man at breakfast yesterday

91

morning told me this. He said he was in charge of a transportation wagon, and had a number of natives as transport riders, and they got to stealing things from the wagon.

He talked to them seriously about it and the next morning, he was poisoned by the natives. The poison was taken from deadly snakes and put into his coffee, and for two years and a half he has been the most dreadful sufferer. The devil seemed as if he had entered into him, presumably through the poison.

When he would come across a snake in the Veldt, it affected him so that he would become apparently paralyzed, and was unable to assist himself. He said that at night he would sometimes wake up choking and could see the devils sitting around him and on his body. Others of the family were also able to discern the presence of hellish powers.

One night he was choking to death and as he lay strangling he saw three devils, sitting on the side of his bed grinning at him. At the same instance he saw a young woman walk into his room praying in a strange language, rebuking these devils, who instantly fled at the name of Jesus and his strangling ceased.

"The next Sunday he was at a meeting in the neighborhood. A young lady whose name I have forgotten now came to him and said, 'Brother, the other night I was awakened and the Lord made me pray most earnestly for you, and as I prayed I became conscious that I was in your room. I walked into the room.

The Lord prayed through me in tongues. I saw three devils sitting on the side of your bed, and you were strangling, choking. The Lord through me rebuked the devils, who fled, and you ceased choking.' 'Now,' she said, 'I don't understand, for I supposed I was in your room, but after a time I found I was still in my own room in my father's house.' These farms where these two people lived were 15 miles apart.

"I could chat here until tomorrow morning and tell you of such incidents as this and other wonderful things that are transpiring every day. The Spirit of God is moving in a deep and wonderful way. The people are beginning to realize that this is God the Almighty.

"In a letter from a native man yesterday, whose face I have never seen he writes me that in the last two months the Lord has given him, in one locality, a church of 100 members (the natives always speak of saved people who come into baptism as members) and in another district the same brother reports 30 members. I give you these instances to let you know how the Lord is taking hold of natives as well as whites.

"One poor native brother, a Zulu in Vatal has been endeavoring to get a church built for the last year piece by piece. He finally got to where he just needed the iron for the roof, and at Bloemfontein conference he told with tears how much they needed that church. Another poor native fellow has been preaching and interpreting for us for a year. He is the man who walked 226 miles to get us to visit his town when we were in the O. R. C. on our first trip! He was turned out of the location because of his inability to pay the native rental of __ shillings per month.

This the municipalities of Africa demand from every native man living in a native location. You can imagine, brother, what it means to me and to him to be able to help these dear men. Another brother who has been faithful __ the work, night and day, ever since we came to Africa, a white brother, has got into financial distress, and his wife called to tell me they were to be turned out of their home because they could not pay their months rent of $15. God tells me to pay that also. These are but a few items of what God is doing in Africa at this time.

LATEST NEWS FROM AFRICA
DECEMBER 1908

God has wonderfully blessed the work here in South Africa. Manifestations of the Spirit have been intense in their power and depth of character beyond anything I have known. Some of the most striking things have occurred. Two weeks ago two-thirds of the congregation—the entire hall being filled—were prostrate under the power of God at one time, saint and sinner alike. Such confessions of sin, even of crimes, I have never before witnessed.

At one meeting we laid hands on I think not less than forty persons for healing and the baptism. The sick were instantly healed and the power of God came upon them in such a degree they fell on the floor and lay under the power for hours. The same thing occurred with those for whom we prayed for the baptism. Bro. Lehman and I believe that 75 percent of the people we have prayed for have been instantly healed.

This morning we were called to pray for a dying woman given up to die of pneumonia. God instantly healed her, and when I left the house, her pain was all gone, her fever had disappeared, and she was perfectly well, though weak. It has been so every day. We have been having conversions and sanctifications at every service, and a great many have received their baptism. In fact, it is the most wonderful Apostolic Faith work I have yet seen.

The seats in the Zion Tabernacle where we are now conducting services on Sunday evenings, are not only filled, but hundreds stand throughout the entire service, and on week nights the seats are filled and usually large numbers have to stand. I have never before had such messages from the Lord as I have received this week. The message on Wednesday night was the most remarkable the Lord has ever spoken through me. It was a message to the Jews. From 200 to 300 Jews attend every service. The message was from the 22nd Psalm, Zechariah 12:10, see also Zechariah 13:6, Luke 2, and the 1st chapter of Revelations.

I am conscious that the prayers of the saints at home are being answered in our behalf in a might manner. I have but one desire in my soul, and that is to do the whole will of God. Missionaries, who have lived here ever since the town was commenced to build thirty-five years ago, assure us every day that Johannesburg was never so religiously stirred before.

John G. Lake

39 Van Beek St., Doonfontein, Johannesburg

An Education In Faith

Reprinted from "The Pentecost"

There is no education in faith like seeing God do the thing. I have a conviction that you can pray and pray and pray until Jesus comes, but unless you get up and believe Him for the thing and commence to use what He has given you, you will never know any more, and you really pray yourself into unbelief. The results that God has given us demonstrate this to my mind.

John G. Lake

Transvaal, South Africa

ASLEEP IN JESUS

JANUARY-FEBRUARY 1909, PAGE 4

Just as we are going to press we are in receipt of a letter from Brother John G. Lake, 4 Millbourn Rd., Bertram, Johannesburg, South Africa, one of the party of missionaries who left Indianapolis last April for missionary work in South Africa, that his wife has been called home to be with Jesus. While we felt the loss of our dear sister deeply, and especially does our heart go out for Brother Lake as he is left alone to this Christian warfare, yet we are glad that we shall see her again on that glorious day when this corruption shall put on incorruption and we shall arise together with those who are now asleep to Him to be forever with the Lord. Brother Lake's letter follows:

My Dear Brother Flower and all the dear friends in America:

I write to tell you that my precious wife was called home to heaven, December 22nd, at 9 p. m. I was absent in the Orange Free State holding native conferences in connection with Brother Inahon, when I received a telegram from Allie, my oldest son, saying, "Mamma is ill, come." I took the first train but she was dead when I got home. Horace (14) and Johnnie (4) were mixed up in a bicycle accident a month ago and were knocked unconscious for quite a long time. Both recovered, but the shock seemed to take hold of Mrs. Lake so she could not eat properly after I had gone away on my last trip. She wrote me Friday, Dec. 18, saying that she was not very well but urging me to remain until the conference closed and I received a little rest.

That evening she sat on the porch late, took a chill, rheumatic fever developed, and before she or our friends or anyone realized she was really ill, it went to her heart and she was dead. She just went to sleep and never woke up here. Oh! I cannot express what it means to us with our seven babies, but Alexander, my oldest son (16) has been such a strength to me in this trial. I cannot explain the marvelous way the dear Lord has used Mrs. Lake here. Her spiritual life, that was always deep and clear, seemed to deepen and deepen into God day by day until she seemed for months to be more on the other side than this.

More people have been baptized under her ministry here than any one of the party. As her dear body lay in our home, the people whom God had blessed, saved and healed, and baptized, came in hundreds to offer a last token of love. One woman, who was blind and healed four weeks ago when Mrs. Lake prayed for her, came to kiss the dear cold hands. Another, the wife of one of the large merchants, who was healed when dying of appendicitis at the Kensington Sanatorium, and many, many more [came]. I mention these cases as they are exceptionally pathetic ones.

I can only go on and trust God. However, I am determined, by God's help, not to permit the children to be scattered. We will maintain our home at all hazards; but oh, beloved, only those who have known our stormy life know the loss that has come to me. In all our battles whether the devil roared or the world frowned or hissed or fawned at our feet, she was just the same, and while I cannot understand His ways in permitting her to leave my side, my faith is unshaken, my confidence is in Him and I am going forward. But the problems that were large before are larger now.

On Tuesday night, at the close of the cottage meeting at our home, Miss Radford, a missionary from Natal, was baptized and spoke in tongues as Mrs. Lake and she prayed together. It was a great anxiety to her that any member of our household should not be baptized by Jesus with the Holy Ghost. When Miss Radford was baptized, she was the last of those who worked with us in our home work except Pete, the native kitchen boy, a young man of twenty-five years. About four hours before she left us, she sent for Pete to come and pray. As he knelt at her bedside, she put her hands on his head and prayed and Jesus baptized him, and when Miss Radford returned to her bedside, Mrs. Lake and Pete were both speaking and praying in tongues.

The Dutch people here called her "The Missus who Prays." They come inquiring for the "Missus Who Prays" yet. Oh, dear ones, do bear me and our family up in your prayers.

I cannot stop, I must go on.

Two months ago, one day as I sat at the desk, she was standing near me. I was looking at the marvelous spirituality of her face when she suddenly turned, and kissing me, said, "Poor Jack, you did not know you brought me to Africa to die, did you?" Then she kissed me quickly and was gone before I realized the import of what it meant. Though I was hundreds of miles away, I knew, through the spirit, what was transpiring, though I could not reach her.

Her life was a sacrifice for others. During the awful press of this work, when we were worn out for want of sleep, she would come and say, "Now Jack, you go to bed and let me pray with the rest of these people," and though I had no special liberty to leave home the last time, she made the arrangements so that I was practically forced to go. She hoped I would return rested. Oh, I feel that she gave her life for others. Dear ones at Indianapolis, you knew her. You will pray for me I know. Also the other dear friends in America.

Your Brother in Jesus, our coming, conquering King,

John G. Lake

P.S. The last vision Jesus gave her was just a short time before she fell into her final sleep. She said to Sister Tom, "Oh, I see a beautiful pure white marble cross." The boys and myself are determined we will have a small white marble cross for her grave. She is buried in Braamfontein Cemetery, Johannesburg, South Africa.

Brother Tom was absent in Pretoria at the time of her death, also Alexander, Horace and Otto, our oldest sons. She never knew she was going apparently. She never said a word about it to anyone. She just fell asleep in Jesus

"The Upper Room" Letters October 1909

Brothers Lake and Hezmalhalch

Brothers John G. Lake and Tom Hezmalhalch from South Africa are now with us at the Upper Room Mission and God is greatly blessing their ministry, and the messages. Brother Tom arrived from Chicago October 8th, and Brother Lake October 29th. The Gospel through them has not been in Word only but in power; and God has borne witness to it with signs following. Some remarkable cases of healing as well as of salvation, and the Pentecostal baptism have taken place.

One Monday evening at the German meeting, a sister was instantly healed of cancer. At the same service, another sister who had a long-standing throat trouble, was waiting at the altar to be prayed for; and whilest Brother Tom was speaking to the audience, she was instantly healed without even a prayer being offered or hands laid upon her. Last Sunday an old brother testified at the close of the day that it was the first time he had been able to hear preaching for years without the use of an ear trumpet. For these and many other manifestations of His mighty power we give God all the glory.

God is certainly with these dear brethren and they surely have His endorsement. His power and glory rest upon them. It is indeed blessed to hear from their lips the mighty work, which God is doing in South Africa. The half has not yet been told. We are indeed glad to find that in spirit we are in real unity with them. And we feel God has linked us together—the Upper Room and the Apostolic Faith work in South Africa

Brother John G. Lake with Brother Tom Hezmalhalch and six others sailed from New York for South Africa, January 15th. Among them were Mr. And Mrs. Moffatt, brother Lake's sister and her husband, and Miss Wicks, who was with us at the Upper Room in November. We will not forget to pray for these precious workers and for the work in South Africa, which is so dear to our hearts.

Before they sailed Brother Lake and Brother Tom both wrote to us telling some very encouraging news which has been coming of the work in Africa. Yet there were also things which seemed to call for their returning at this time, earlier than we had expected. Brother Lake, however, feels that he will be back in this country, at no very distant date, for a more extended tour in the States and in Canada.

"The Upper Room" Updates

September-October 1910

Entry One:

We are very glad to be able to report such encouraging news of the work in South Africa. During the past two months we have received letters from various sources and different districts of that vast field, and from them it is evident that in spite of the fierce opposition of the devil and the failures of men, God is moving wonderfully and mighty works are being wrought in the name of Jesus. This is true of the work in Johannesburg as well as in other parts of the country, including Cape Colony, Orange River Colony and Basutoland. Our latest news, (a personal letter from which we quote on page 8) told us that Brother Tom had gone to Cape Colony and Brother Lake was at the Central Tabernacle in Johannesburg for awhile.

Entry Two:

Brother Lake has sent us an urgent call to prayer for a projected campaign in Basutoland, which is a native state of about 250,000 population. God has opened a wide door to our Apostolic Faith Mission to enter there; and in fact an entrance and a good start have already been made.

GOD'S MIGHTY MOVINGS IN AFRICA

Writing on the Veldt near Ladybrand (Orange River Colony) on April 23rd, Brother John G. Lake tells us of the wonderful way in which God is working as follows:

"I came over here on the Basutoland border after closing our Annual Native Conference at Bloemfontein last Tuesday; this is Saturday noon. We began European meetings the instant we arrived and the people have come in carts and on horseback for many miles, bringing their food with them. It is really a little camp-meeting.

"The Baptism of the Holy Ghost is falling in great power. Last night two sisters received the baptism in the meeting, and after retiring, the Spirit fell on them again and all night they sang the praises of God. Oh, it is glorious! A brother was baptized the day before yesterday, and God has marvelously used him since. And this morning at our praise service a Dutch sister received her baptism and broke forth in tongues, praising God in an ecstasy of joy.

"In answer to prayer God has raised up a Brother Hartman as white superintendent of our Basutoland work. He with his wife who has the baptism also, will

109

travel in an African ox wagon which will be their only home. He made a trip into the interior some time ago and the Pentecostal power fell at one native church, since which the native minister writes that a hundred sick heathen have come to be prayed for and have been healed. It is wonderful how the real old Gospel with healing reaches the native heart.

"Sometimes as I look at the vastness of the work which God has put into our hands, I long to be able to spend all my time in native work exclusively. One of the chiefs in Basutoland has offered to build us a house and give us land to cultivate if we will come and minister to the blacks alone: and sometimes I truly wish it were possible. But God must decide: I cannot. Nevertheless, it is in my heart.

"I left Schwede at Bloemfontein where God started a fine European meeting. Sixteen Europeans had been saved when I left, and many wonderful healings. One insane man was delivered by God, and a crippled woman healed. Last Sunday night, the power of God fell mightily on the conference and many were saved and healed. Very many natives were also saved. Bless God. Bless God!

"Last night a Salvation Army officer, Mrs. ___ was instantly healed of long-standing rheumatism that had made her knees stiff: and a boy paralyzed on one side was also healed at once, the contraction of the chords and muscles relapsed and his hand became straight. I could go on telling you of the wonderful things which God is doing, but I must close.

"It is the beginning of winter now; the Veldt is brown and the nights cold, but no frost yet. I am sitting by an African river, only a stream 3 feet wide and 3 inches deep now but in summer it is a mighty river. I can see over into Basutoland and hope to be there soon. The Holy Ghost yesterday told us where we were to labor there. It was like the church at Antioch (Acts 13:2-4): it was wonderful. These Dutch people are very sweet when softened by the Spirit, loving and warm-hearted.

"'The Mid-Africa Review,' a Dutch secular magazine at Johannesburg, now publishes six pages per issue of our material. Glory to God. That shows the public interest which God has aroused in South Africa: for news is what the people want to read and what this magazine finds it profitable to print. May America also find such an interest in God's work. God bless you. Send us all the Upper Room papers you can afford."

At Ladybrand, where I ministered to the European Assembly, the dear Lord baptized half of the Assembly, and raised up four excellent workers. One of them, Brother Hartman, accompanied me with two native workers to Kessliroad, Witsieshoek and _____.

This document is not complete. The remainder was illegible.

More News From South Africa

We quote the following items from some of the recent letters we have received from Brother Lake. They surely show that our God is working still in a wonderful way in different part of South Africa.

Writings from Somerset East, in Cape Colony, on June 14th, Brother Lake says: "I am sitting on a rock overlooking the town of Somerset East, which lies in the valley with a beautiful crescent-shaped mountain, 4000 feet high, for a background. This part of the country is very beautiful, and has some things that are new to me, for instance, the wild aloes with half a dozen bright red flowers 12 inches long and so thick that a whole mountain side will be brilliant with red. This is also a great ostrich-raising district and the farmers of the locality are wealthy. The country is wooded with the native thorn bush or thorn tree, and it is good to see a green tree of any kind in this veldt country. In fact, the general appearance around here is similar to Northern California.

"At Cookhouse, thirty miles from here, we have a beautiful work. It started while I was in Los Angeles last year, and now 100 have been baptized by Christian baptism, most of them wealthy landowners. And

113

already in one family, the Watsons, the dear Lord has called five brothers into this work, and they are amongst the best leaders we have. To show you how God works, one of these Watson brothers was a wild fellow and ran away from home and went north in the Transvaal to Louis-Trichardt. There William Duggan came with his wonderful ministry of healing and sanctification, and this man Watson got saved and baptized with the Holy Ghost. Bless God, that wonderful faith-fire, which was in Duggan's heart, burned its way into Watson's also: in fact, Duggan's converts seem to possess his wonderful faith spirit. It reminds me of what God said to Moses when He commanded him to ordain the 70 elders, 'Take thou of the Spirit that is upon thee and put it upon them.'

"After Watson was saved, he came back to his old home and told his brothers what God had done for him: and now he and his four brothers are all in this work. Praise God, is it not wonderful! The fruits to date are 100 baptized, most of them English colonials (some Dutch), and a mighty fire is burning through the whole district. Now the work has spread through them to Somerset East: and here a dear brother who was a great drunkard, about 37 years old, was saved; then he came to Johannesburg where he got baptized with the Holy Ghost and has returned to preach the Gospel.

Now Brother Vandewall and I are here and we believe that God is going to raise up a glorious work. Oh, Brother, God seems to have made me to water this work

114

with my tears, but bless God, it is taking root all around the land. The Cookhouse congregation is going to build a church, which will be the first Apostolic Faith Mission Church built in Africa by Europeans. The Vrededorp congregation at Johannesburg has bought a wood and iron building and is paying for it on easy payments. God is working in His own way all around. In these little towns and villages you cannot rent a hall as you can in America, for there are none to rent: so when we get crowded out of a dwelling we have to get some kind of a meeting house."

From Port Elizabeth, Cape Colony, July 4th.

"I am just leaving here for Barkley Bridge where our workers from Orange River Colony and Basutoland are having a convention for three days. God is moving there more wonderfully among the whites than He has done in Southern Africa before. The natives, too, are being saved and healed in great numbers. I get almost daily reports from some part of that field. My own brother, Wilford, is proving an admirable missionary: he has got the grit to endure and presently when he has had two years' experience in the field, he will do finely.

"The idea which some have that natives can Christianize themselves is, I am sure, a mistake. All undeveloped natives retrograde fast when let alone. It takes the better energy of the white man to stir them to activity; of course Letwaba is an exception for he is equal to many white workers.

"I have been here ten days. At first we only had one person in sympathy with our work; but God has raised up a nice company of Dutch and English workers and I leave them settled as an assembly and moving on fast. The Baptism of the Holy Ghost fell last night. Bless God."

Bloemfontein. July 5th.

"At Barkley Bridge I visited some of our dear saints and a young man, a relative of the family, who had been absent on a trip to buy donkeys and had visited a back settlement over the mountains known as the Karoo said to me: 'I'm no Christian myself, and I don't take any personal interest in your religion, but I tell you what I found up in the Karoo. I used to go there and it was a tough place with plenty of devil there: but this time, as soon as I would get into a house, they wanted to get the Bible down and show me things you teach. I tell you it has turned that district upside down.' You may imagine how my heart rejoiced at this news.

"I want your earnest prayers for a great battle is in progress. The churches on every hand seem to be combined to crush this work: fighting is hard and thick and laborers few. But oh, bless God, to find 100 saved and the blessed work going on with vim is good and, once more, demonstrates how God the Holy Ghost evangelizes.

Here these local workers have risen up strong, practical, saved, baptized men and women without any help from headquarters. Until now they have depended entirely upon God and gone forward; and now God's Spirit is being poured out on the district and many souls are coming to God. These brethren are mostly ostrich farmers and they travel long distances from farm to farm and district to district to carry this glorious Gospel. As I told you before the work has started through the conversion of Watson under William Duggan in Louis-Trichardt."

Maseru, Basutoland, July 12th.

"Our work has so spread through this territory that some Basutoland center is a necessity now, and negotiations with the government and with the chiefs are under way, but it is a slow process and requires much patience which it is difficult for an American to exercise. The rule in Africa is pretty much, 'If we don't arrive this year, why, well, we will get there next year anyway.' But as the consciousness of the Lord's near return is upon us, one is disposed to press matters and to work rather than to pray. How glad I am that God has taught me to pray as I run and run as I pray.

"We are finding the need of pressing our white work this year, for the native work has grown to such proportions that we must have many, many more white workers and God is laying such a missionary spirit upon these white converts that they quickly get into native work. It is wonderful to see, as we have in some instances, the dear Lord take almost half an assembly and separate them to His work.

THE COMPOUND WORK

"We have instituted this year native compound work. At each of the mines here, they have a great native compound, the home of the natives who work on the mine. During the time of contract with the mines, they are not permitted to wander about the city but are confined to these compounds. They are large squares with living rooms all along the outside and an open center. Our audience in one compound last Sunday numbered about 400 natives. I do not think that anywhere in the world there is such an opportunity for evangelistic work, as the ___ Rand presents.

"There are hundreds and thousands of natives from all over South Africa in these compounds. Their labor contract is always at least six months, and is sometimes renewed for another six months, then they go back to their homes and fresh ones take their place. This goes on continuously. When you go out on the Veldt, you

118

must travel great distances between villages and farms, from one audience to another, but here you have them already concentrated into audiences for you.

"I expect to visit Roodepoort today and arrange with the compound manager of one of the mines for the exclusive right of our mission to minister to the natives in their compound. We have not been able to even touch this work, but the faithfulness of a few of the saints of America has made possible this opening of this new branch of our work.

A Word of Warning

"American missionaries as a rule have not proven a success in this work in South Africa. The Dutch people are extremely conservative on religious lines. Their ministers exercise a great dominion over them very similar to the Roman Catholic priesthood of Ireland. No American so far, except Brother Tom and myself, has been able to break through and accomplish anything among the Dutch.

"Another thing, Brother, this movement is committed to the strong teaching of Divine healing and manifestations of the Spirit. The missionaries who have come from America, instead of coming in an attitude to be taught, most of them have come expecting to teach the people here. They are far behind the people here in the exercise of active faith in God. Their ministry has not proven a blessing. Instead of rising up to the standard that God has set here, many of them have endeavored to pull the standard down to their level, and this has caused great friction.

"The Dutch brethren have come to me this week and suggested that I embody in a letter to the missions of America these facts. That is the reason that I am writing as I am. The women missionaries who have been much blessed and used of God, Miss Wick, Mrs. Watson, Miss Vera Barnard, Miss Edith Zader, Miss Ida Sackett and dear Mother Tom Hezmalhalch. The women apparently come to work for Jesus and get souls saved, not to grind axes. I have asked the brethren who waited on me to do their own writing on this subject themselves, so you may hear from them later.

"There is a broad field in Africa for any man or any woman who will only take his place in God's ranks for the salvation of souls, but the situation in Africa is very complicated on account of the racial prejudices that exist here. Unless one has been a student of conditions here before coming over, it takes a long time to get on the inside of these things where one can work effectively.

"Among the natives there are great tribe jealousies, and the only thing that prevents open war between them is the strong hand of the British government. There is also the strong prejudice between the Dutch and English that has existed in America after the Civil War. All these things have to be overcome. Africa is not an easy field, but in my judgment, the very hardest field there is anywhere, especially on these particular lines. Nevertheless, God is moving mightily and is continuously raising up strong men right on the ground who carry forward this

Gospel. No less than 30 new Dutch evangelists have come into the work in the past five months. These have been raised right in the country and understand all the conditions and speak the languages, always Dutch, English and at least one native language, in most cases. Consequently, Brother, they are able to minister to all classes and intermingled audiences.

"God bless dear Brother Fisher and yourself. I never cease to pray for you and for all the dear saints in the Upper Room."

John G. Lake

SANCTIFICATION
AND
HOLY LIVING

JUNE 1909

As I have seen that there is much confusion and apparent misconception of the teaching of sanctification and the teaching of holy living as taught by some of the advanced teachers, I feel compelled to write a short article calling attention to the actual difference in this teaching, believing that it may be a blessing to others who have tried to live a holy life and really practice holy living to the best of their ability and have been unable to satisfy their own hearts that their present experience is in the will of God.

Salvation, healing and holy living has been the standard of Christian teaching among many, and many have struggled to live a holy life who have found it impossible to be holy according to the Bible standard and their own conscience. This article is written in the hope that these may be able to see and enter into the real inwrought experience of a real sanctified life in God; that will make it possible for them to live a holy life.

Holy living as taught among modern Christian teachers has meant that in our outward everyday living we shall imitate the life of Christ; that we shall be clean men and clean women; that the purity of our life shall be unquestionable; that in all our acts we shall act like Christ.

This is really Christian ethics and is not scriptural holiness. Holiness of heart and ethics are very closely connected. They correlate and interact. Their right adjustment and mutual development is the problem before us.

At one time in the world's history ethics was exalted above inward experience as though purity of heart was caused by holy living. This has been the great error. At another time inward experience was exalted above ethics as though purity of heart existed independent of holy living. For two hundred years the pendulum has swung, first to the one extreme, then to the other. Both of these theories come of limited one-sided views of Christianity; the former obtained before the Wesleyan reformation.

Thomas A Kempis in his book, "The Imitation of Christ," was the first great teacher of holy living. Excepting the Bible, this book is declared to have been translated more often and more widely read than any other book. It is said to have reached five hundred editions. This book was published in the latter half of the fourth century. In 1650, Bishop Jeremy Taylor published his "Holy Living and Dying." This followed in the line of "The Imitation of Christ."

Following Jeremy Taylor's "Holy living and Dying," seventy-five years later, came William Law's "Serious Call to a Devout and Holy Life,' and his "Practical Treatise Upon Christian Perfection."

These books are the foundation of the teaching of holy living and are written from the standpoint of Christian ethics. They emphasize purity of heart, but fail to particularize the act of faith by which the heart is cleansed from sin. "And put no difference between us and them, purifying their hearts by faith." (Acts 15:9) "To open their eyes, and to turn them from darkness to light, and from the power of Satan unto God, that they may receive forgiveness of sins, and inheritance among them which are sanctified by faith that is in me." (Acts 26:18)

Nor God's act of faith by which the heart is instantly cleansed from indwelling sin. "Knowing this, that our old man is crucified with him, that the body of sin might be destroyed, that henceforth we should not serve sin." (Rom. 6:6) "For the law of the Spirit of life in Christ Jesus hath made me free from the law of sin and death." (Rom. 8:2)

"And the very God of peace sanctify you wholly; and I pray God your whole spirit and soul and body be preserved blameless unto the coming of our Lord Jesus Christ." (1 Thess. 5:23) They bent their force upon holy living and this left the impression that purity of heart would result from holy living. Influenced by these books, John and Charles Wesley in 1729 followed after holiness and incited others to do so.

In 1737, they saw likewise that men are justified before they are sanctified. (Methodist Discipline, page 13.) Here it appears that John Wesley aimed at holy living for eight years before he ever saw that he must be first sanctified by the blood of Jesus before he could be holy either in heart or life. How many of us have made the same error? How many of us have tried and tried to live a holy life with the old nature of sin still in our breast? When the heart is purified from all sin then the outer life will manifest it.

Is it any wonder that people failed when the author of "Holy Living and Dying" did not even profess justification? He says on pages 292-3, "A true penitent must all the days of his life pray for pardon and never think the work completed until he dies.... and whether God hath forgiven us or no, we know not."

In the face of this teaching, the clear cut teaching of John Wesley on the nature of entire sanctification wrought in an instant by a divine act conditioned alone upon a specific act of sanctifying faith in the Blood of Christ, followed by endless growth in holiness of heart and life, stands forth in marvelous grandeur.

In fact, for putting the clear evenly balanced, well-rounded, all-including, ever-abounding scriptural holiness, John Wesley has no equal. With him as with us, holiness was "having the mind of Christ" and walking as Christ also walked, even having not some part only but all the mind which was in Him and walking as He walked, not only in many or most respects, but in all things, so that the purpose of God is really made a fact in our lives. (See Eph. 1:4) "According as he hath chosen us in him before the foundation of the world that we should be holy and without blame before him in love."

"And you, that were sometime alienated and enemies in your mind by wicked works, yet now hath he reconciled in the body of his flesh through death, to present you holy and unblameable and unreproveable in his sight." (Col. 1:21, 22)

Oh, glory!

He can do it, He can do it.

He has done it for me.

Hallelujah! Hallelujah!

SOUTH AFRICA
AND BROTHER LAKE

We feel the time has come for us to speak out more clearly and definitely than we have hitherto done in regard to Brother John G. Lake and the work in South Africa.

It has been our privilege to be in very close touch with this work and to hear both sides of the question. Whereas some of our readers and the editors of other Pentecostal papers have, for the most part, heard only one side of the accusations, which have been made against Brother Lake. We are in correspondence with a number of people in South Africa: some of these we know personally: we have touched their lives (in close touch), we know their spirit and have good reason to believe what they write to us.

In addition to this, we can say that very carefully and urgently with open mind wanting only to know God's will, we have waited upon Him until we know that we heard from Him—and that more than once. For we realized the responsibility before God of taking the stand we were taking and of publishing the reports which we have done when other workers were accusing Brother Lake and trying to detract from the work which he is doing, or rather which God is doing through him.

We may be grieved, and we confess we are, at the tremendous opposition and the accusations that have been made against Brother Lake, but we are not surprised at it. For most assuredly God is dong a wonderful work in South Africa today and it is spread over a large portion of that subcontinent too; and He, the Lord, has set up Brother Lake in the place of leadership, which hundreds of the best workers there fully recognize and are loyally and lovingly working with him.

God has been able to manifest His mighty power in healing and in salvation on a large scale there in South Africa, perhaps on a larger scale than anywhere else in the world. Real miracles of healing have been and are being constantly wrought in the name and power of Jesus Christ, as great as any recorded in apostolic days (to God be all the glory!) And these miracles of healing have forced men to see the reality and power of the Gospel, and have stirred them to seek God and to come to the Apostolic Faith Mission all over South Africa. Small wonder then that the devil has combined forces in hell and on earth to overthrow this work and to discredit God's leader.

We speak confidently and advisedly on this matter, for we know whereof we speak before God, and we are sure of our ground. We are writing in this strain because of open letters and some private letters which have been sent to this country from South Africa making serious charges against Brother Lake. It was because of these accusations that we were entirely silent about the work over there in our August issue. We wanted to be assured from God of the truth of these things and what He expected of us in the matter, and it was not until we had heard from Him again (as well as hearing from other correspondents on the field) that we began to publish afresh reports of the work there.

(1) One of these accusations against Brother Lake was that he had misappropriated funds, which had been sent to him from this country for the work. Brother Lake has written to several that by far the largest part of the monies received by him from America had come through the Upper Room Mission, and I know that we have sent to him since April 1st a little over $2200, besides sending considerable funds to Brothers Schwede and Letwaba for the workers in South Africa.

We sent it to Brother Lake with no conditions attached (except that it was not to be used for buying land, for building, or for secular education), because we had every confidence in his integrity and his ability to administer the money wisely and well for the work there. We have even greater confidence in him today, and if we had $1000 in our hands now, we would be very glad to send it to him.

We have received a report of how the monies have been expended from the Treasurer of the Apostolic Faith Mission in Johannesburg, Mr. Peter Moffitt, and we are perfectly satisfied that the funds have been well and carefully spent and the very great things have been accomplished in spreading this precious Pentecostal Gospel over a wide area of South Africa.

In that country distances are great and railroad fares expensive and some of the dear workers there, when they had not enough money for railroad fares, have walked over the burning veldt (sometimes with bleeding feet) in order to take the Gospel to needy districts which were calling for help.

(2) Another charge has been made that Brother Lake had failed to keep promises, which he had made to send money to support native workers. Well, if he has failed, (I don't know that he has), I believe God will hold us in the homeland more grievously at fault than Brother Lake because we have not sent funds more generously where He is working so mightily: and even more responsible, we believe, God will hold those men who by their evil reports from South Africa have stopped the flow of funds from this country.

(3) As to exaggerated reports, which it is alleged, have been sent, we can only say that from the letters which we receive constantly from different parts of that country, we believe in many cases there has been understatement rather than overstatement of what God has been doing.

(4) It has been charged that Brother Lake was ambitious to be The Great Chief of all the work, and exercising the spirit of "boss" ("a second Dowie," one wrote). As to this we will say that when it first came to us several months ago, we took all Brother Lake's recent letters written to us (and they were many) and before re-reading them carefully, we waited upon God asking Him to show us through them "between the lines," if not in the actual words, the wrong spirit of the writer, if he had a wrong spirit: and we are free to confess that in them we found nothing but the same generous, warm-hearted, forgiving and humble spirit that we had felt and seen in him when he was with us last year for a full month, when we were in the closest touch with him and in intimate fellowship night and day continually: and at first in those days we were inclined to watch him critically as one who had been so written and spoken against.

Perhaps I have written enough, but one word more I must say that Brother E. K. Fisher and many others of our faithful workers in the Upper Room Mission, who know about this matter and who also know how to pray until they hear from God, fully endorse what I have written.

George B. Studd

THE AFRICAN DIARY
OF JOHN G. LAKE

FORWARD

The African diary of John G. Lake is a record of God's use and dealings with a man who continues to speak to the generations that have followed him.

Through the years, Dr. Lake's sermons and writings have been a source of great inspiration to me as well as to countless others. This diary recounts the trials, triumphs, and the tragedies that he found in Africa. By reading his later works, one can hear the cry of his heart for another chance at a crusade that would rival the magnitude of the revival started in Africa by the arrival of a small group of American missionaries who had sold everything they had just to get there.

During Lake's time in Africa he, along with several other missionaries, were responsible under God for the birthing of over 125 "white" churches and over 500 "native" churches. While reading this document, keep in mind that Dr. Lake continued his work in Africa even after losing his wife only 6 months after their arrival. Dr. Lake also had his five children with him. Even with all of this "going against him," he managed to set the course for Africa and wrote the South African National Constitution. As you read this work, pray that God will use you to stir a nation as Dr. Lake stirred Africa.

God bless you,
Rev. Curry R. Blake, General Overseer
John G. Lake Ministries & International Apostolic Council

BAPTIZED IN THE HOLY GHOST

In October 1907, the Lord in His goodness baptized me with the Holy Ghost, after several months of deep heart searching and repentance unto God, at the home of a friend where I had gone in company with Bro. Thos. Hezmalhalch. I was called at my home at Zion City, Ill., to invite me to accompany him to pray for a sister who was an invalid and had been in a wheel chair for a number of years.

As we entered the home, I felt a great calm resting upon me. I did not feel to join in conversation. Bro. Tom proceeded to instruct the sister from the Word concerning healing, and I sat in a deep leather chair on the opposite side of the room. My soul was drawn out in a great silent heart cry to God. "Oh Jesus, I so long for the Baptism of the Holy Ghost, but I feel so unworthy, so far from thee. Oh, Christ, if it be possible to baptize such as me, please baptize me.

"I am so hungry, so tired of trying, so weary of doing things myself. I am sick of sin, sick of self, sick of trying, sick of working, etc., etc." Presently, a great quiet came upon me, deepening rapidly into a peace such as I had never before known or experienced.

A quiet of spirit, soul, and body; my being was soothed in a perfect calm so deep so quiet my mind was perfectly still. I said, "Oh, Jesus, what is this calm of God? Is this the Baptism of the Holy Ghost?" Presently, it seemed as if I had passed under a warm, tropical rain that was falling not upon me but through me. The realization of peace was such as I had never known. The rain continued to fall upon me. Oh, the rest of soul. Oh, the quiet of God. Oh, the peace of that hour; the peace I cannot describe that passeth all understanding. This condition of peace was so great, I feared to breathe. It was as the silence of heaven.

The running rain continued to fall upon me: it soothed my brain; it soothed my body; it soothed my spirit. Would it ever stop? I feared it might. I said, "Oh, God, I did not know there was such a place of rest as this."

Then I became conscious of a change coming over me; instead of the rain, currents of power running through me from my head to my feet, seemingly into the floor. These shocks of power came intermittently, possibly 10 seconds apart. They increased in voltage until after a few minutes my frame shook and vibrated under these mighty shocks of power. Then, as I shook and trembled, the shocks of power following each other with more apparent rapidity and intensity, my forehead became sealed, my brain in the front portion of my head became inactive, and I realized the Spirit speaking of His seal in their foreheads.

140

I would have fallen on the floor, except for the depth of the chair in which I sat. Again a charge of shocks of power lessened in intensity and now a power took hold of my lower jaw. It moved up and down and sideways in a manner new to me. My tongue and throat began to move in a manner I could not control. Presently, I realized I was speaking in another tongue, a language I had never learned. Oh, the sense of power, the mighty moving of the Spirit in me, the consciousness it was God who had come. Then Satan came and suggested it is not real power, it is only imagination, these are not currents of real power, it is only psychic phenomena. I said, "It's power, I know it," and God in loving mercy proved it to me.

At this point Bro. Tom, not yet having observed what the Lord had been doing with me, motioned me to come to pray with the sick woman. As I stood up, I was trembling so violently, I was afraid to put my hands upon her head. Knowing the honeycombed state of the bone in many Rheumatic cripples, I was afraid, lest the trembling of my body might dislocate the rigid neck. It occurred to me to touch the top of her head with the tips of my fingers only, permitting the joints of my fingers to work thus no jar to the sick one was necessary.

As I touched her head, I could feel the currents of power shoot through me into her. Bro. Tom was still so engaged with the sister, he had not yet observed that Jesus had baptized me. I opened my mouth wide thus not permitting the moving of my tongue to produce sound. Presently, Bro. Tom said, "Let us pray," at the same instant taking one of the sister's hands. At that instant, a shock of power shot through me and down through the sister into Bro. Tom.

He instantly dropped her hand and drew back, apparently not realizing what had happened. He again lifted the hand and started to pray. As he prayed, the Spirit deepened on me. I could keep the sounds back no longer, and as I prayed, the Spirit prayed through me in another tongue unknown to me. For years I had been used of God in laying hands on the sick. God had given me wonderful healings at times, but there was no running continuity of healing power. As I prayed, the Spirit said, "What shall I give you?" I said, "Oh, Jesus, my soul has coveted the gift of healing," and I felt that thenceforth God would use me in that ministry.

Following my Baptism in the Holy Ghost, came six months of the most terrible fightings, sometimes victory, sometimes defeat, sometimes awful clouds and soul storms with glimpses of God's sunshine. The Spirit talked to me of giving up all. I did not know what that would mean, but oh, brothers and sisters, when we say, "All to Jesus," it means much: my home, business, position among men, friends, family. Even my dear wife could not at this time understand.

God said, "Go and preach." I said, "I will, nights, but I must go on with my business." After some months, I found my interest in commercial and worldly affairs was passing away. A man would come into my office, I could not think of his money. I could only think of his soul—Oh, was he saved? Could I bring him Jesus?—and many times it ended in my telling him of this wonderful salvation and kneeling to pray instead of talking business at all. Oh, beloved, when the Spirit of Jesus, the Holy Ghost comes, it is Jesus' own passion for souls. You must love them; you can't help it. Jesus died for them; the Holy Ghost is His Spirit. He loves them, still He loves them through you.

Again, the Lord said, "Follow me," and like Matthew, I closed my office, arose, and followed Him. Some months before I was baptized, I sat in a cottage meeting at the home of Bro. Fred Bosworth. Bro. Tom was preaching. At the close of the meeting he came to me and said, "Brother, what is your name?" I said, "John Lake." He replied, "John Lake, as I was preaching, Jesus told me you and I are going to preach together." I laughed, replying lightly, "I wish it were so, but I cannot preach. I am not where I ought to be with God."

He said, Never mind, Jesus is going to fix you up." Some months later as he visited our town again, one day I joined Bro. Tom and Bro. Fred Bosworth on the sidewalk. As we walked down the street, I stepped between them, taking each by the arm. Bro. Bosworth turned to me saying, "Lake, when are you going to surrender to Jesus?" I said, "Any time, Fred." Tom turned to me saying, "Do you mean it?" I replied, "I do, Tom." We all three fell on our knees on the sidewalk, and right there I surrendered to my Lord. Then I sought God for sanctification and my Baptism in the Holy Ghost.

One day, about April 1st, 1908, I went to Indianapolis, Indiana for a 10 day visit with Bro. Tom who was preaching there. Then I assisted in the services and work.

While visiting at the home of a Bro. Osborne, as we prayed before retiring, the Spirit of the Lord came upon me and God talked to me concerning Africa. From my childhood, I had been much interested in Africa, especially South Africa, and for years I had felt that one day God would send me to Africa, but never possessing what I regarded as the Divine Equipment necessary for a successful Christian worker. I had banished the thought and stifled the voice within.

Then, I now had a large family—myself, wife, and seven children—the way seemed impossible. God gave me at this time a spiritual vision of Africa, especially of the Zion work there—so accurate, that when I arrived in Africa 14 months later, I found it correct in every detail. As my 10 day visit closed, I found myself being drawn strongly to return at once to my business, but God would not give me liberty to do this. And this has always been, to me, one of the strange workings of God in my life.

My affairs needed my personal attention much. It seemed suicidal to put my complicated business into another's hands to close up. As I said, being overpowered with the desire to return to my office and put my affairs in shape, I decided to do so. And then commenced spiritual and physical chastisement so terrible I felt as though my reason must surely be dethroned while in this turmoil of soul. One day, I met Bro. Pearse, now of Australia; a precious godly man. He said, "Bro. Lake, the Lord has been laying it on my heart to invite you to come to my home that we may have an evening of prayer together." I said, "I will come tonight."

At 8 p.m. I was there. Bro. Pearce's wife and daughter and myself made up the praying company. As we knelt to pray, my soul was in such anguish I felt myself being overshadowed by the Holy Spirit, then commenced the most vivid spiritual experience of my life. The Lord brought to my remembrance from my childhood on every occasion when He had tried to woo me to His way and I had turned to my own way instead.

Oh, the many, many times He had called when I did not heed, times long since forgotten by me. Oh, how He showed me His love for me. He showed me the lost world, dying souls, the sick and suffering, saying, "all this I did for thee, what hast thou done for me?" until my heart broke and, in anguish, I cried and told Him I would go all the way with Him even unto death. Then the Spirit said, "Will you go?" I said, "Yes, Lord, any place, anywhere. But, Oh, Jesus, the burden must be yours, the responsibility is yours."

Then a series of visions of different cities came before me: first, Zion City, Ill., where the Glory of God overshadowed the old Dr. Dowie tabernacle in Shiloh Park as a heavenly light and radiated out over the entire city. Oh, what a spirit of prayer was in me. My soul flowed out in a cry for the lost and perishing world. Then He showed me the downtown district of the city of Indianapolis, Indiana, and the same illumination of God's glory, only in a smaller compass. This is understood to be the extent of God's blessing on each place through our ministry. Then, Johannesburg, South Africa, and a wonderful illumination of God's glory lighting up the whole land. My soul continued to pour out in a stream of prayer.

Then two other places were shown. Again, I heard the voice, "Will you go?" "Yes, yes," I cried, "if You will prepare and equip me and go with me." I prayed, "When will I go?" And at once commenced to roll from my mouth in another tongue a single word, repeated over and over, perhaps twenty times. I said, "Lord, what is it? What does this word mean?" And, at once, the interpretation came—"Indianapolis." I cried, "Lord, I will go, I'll go at once."

When I arose from my knees, it was to find the household in great fear, believing I must have lost my reason. I confronted them, assuring them it was God. On looking at my watch, I was amazed to find I had been on my knees for 4 hours—the first time in my life such a thing had occurred. I returned to my own home and told my dear wife. The Spirit so rested upon me that I spoke in tongues or prayed the entire night.

In the morning, I packed my suitcase and went to Indianapolis, where I joined Bro. Tom in his meetings. As I entered the hall, he said "I knew you were coming. Take a seat here by me." The following night, as I stood to testify, the Spirit impelled me to say, "Bro. Tom thinks he's going to Colorado, but he is not, he is coming to Zion City with me." Tom laughed, "Not unless the Lord sends me." I replied, "You will hear from heaven." Some days later, while he was praying, the Lord told him to go. Oh, what a wonderful series of meetings that was. How God poured out His Spirit. At the meeting in the upper room of Bro. Hammond's Faith Home, the Haven, twenty-five were baptized in the Holy Ghost and spoke in tongues. In perhaps 20 minutes, the Spirit of God fell on the meeting like a cloud.

Instantly, one after another commenced to speak in tongues. Oh what glory, oh what high praises of God,

147

oh what rejoicing! It was estimated that several hundreds received the Baptism of the Holy Ghost during this series of services lasting, I think, in all about 6 months.

One day in October, I went out with a young man to saw down a large oak tree for firewood. I had been praying about guidance for future work for the Lord for some days, believing my mission at Zion City to be fulfilled, when again the Spirit spoke to me and said, "Go to Indianapolis. Rent a large hall. Prepare for a winter campaign, and in the spring, <u>you will go to Africa</u>."

I again obeyed without question. On arriving there, I found a little company of saints holding an occasional meeting in a small hall. I told them what the Lord had said, and God witnessed to them it was His message. We had no money, but we believed God. We prayed, and in a few days had no less than $100 handed in for the Lord's use. We commenced the work in a large hall, and from the first, God greatly blessed in saving, healing, and baptizing many in the Holy Ghost.

An operation of God occurred at this time I feel it good to record. For many months, Bro. Tom and myself had been praying for greater power for the healing of the sick and the casting out of demons at this time.

One morning on coming to breakfast, I found I could not eat, but felt well. At noon it was the same. This continued for days. A great desire to pray came upon me and I could do nothing but pray. On the evening of the 4th or 5th day, as I knelt to pray, the Spirit of God spoke to me and said, "From thenceforth, you shall cast out demons."

On the following night, a young man came to me inquiring, "Do you believe that motto up there?" pointing to a painted motto in large letters on the wall. It was: "In My name shall they cast out devils." I said, "Yes, Brother, I do." He said, "Are you sure, for I am in earnest." I replied, "My Brother, with all the earnestness of my soul, I do." "Well," he replied, "I have a brother in the asylum. He has been there 2 years and the doctors cannot give us any hope or, in fact, seem to be at a loss to explain the reason for his condition."

I then inquired under what circumstances his brother had went insane. He told me that the brother had been attending a revival meeting and was seeking sanctification and was a religious man who had trained his family in the fear of the Lord; that he had suddenly went insane. They had to put him in the asylum. His family was in great financial stress. The Spirit of the Lord impressed me it was a case of devil possession. And we arranged the brother should be brought to the meeting on Sunday afternoon.

He came in charge of his brother and sister and an attendant. He came at once and was persuaded to kneel at the altar. I then called a number of saints whom I knew to be vigorous in faith for healing and casting out demons: Bro. & Sister Flower, their son, Roswell, Miss Alice Reynolds, and others.

Then I stepped down, put my hands on his head, and rebuked, bound, cast the devil out. He was instantly delivered and sat up quietly. Three days after, he was discharged from the asylum and went home well; returned to his work in a grain elevator. Four months afterward, his mother, sister and brother returned to the mission to praise God saying he was perfectly, permanently delivered. The power to cast out demons continues to abide upon me.

When the bumps of life have bumped you 50 years,

When your bumps are sore and new bumps bring the tears,

When the bumps who do the bumping hope that they have

got you jumping, that's the time God bumps the bumpers,

never fear.

When the love glow of your spirit (unfinished)

DIARY ENTRIES
NOV. 24, 1910 – JAN. 2, 1911

THURSDAY, NOVEMBER 24ᵀᴴ, 1910

A remarkable case of casting out a devil took place after the evening service. A Mr. Cornelius, possessed of a devil for about 1 ½ years, said that in a vision God showed him Bro. Gordon Hinds, and said he was to come to our tabernacle and that Bro. Hinds and Bro. Lake would lay hands on him and cast out a devil. We did. As we prayed, he fell backward to top of the platform, then slipped down into a sitting [position] on the floor with his back against the platform.

The devil caused him to cry out and fight with his fists, but in a few minutes he was overpowered by the Holy Ghost and cast out. Throughout the struggle, Bro. Lake held his head firmly between his hands, at the same time in the Name of Jesus commanding the devil to come out, which he did. When the devil was cast out, the glory and praise of Jesus filled his soul. In a few minutes, the Holy Ghost [had] such possession of him he spoke in tongues and praised Jesus and God.

SUNDAY, NOVEMBER 27TH, 1910

A young man who had been ill from sun stroke was brought to the tabernacle from Potchefstroom by Bro. Heboldt. He had suffered for six months with violent pains in his head. The dear Lord healed him as myself and Bro. Vanderwall and Bro. Heboldt prayed and laid hands on him. The morning service was a glorious one indeed. Bless God! The Holy Ghost so moved on people's hearts that the hymns announced the testimonies and messages were all in one spirit and thought as though a programme had been arranged beforehand.

Evening service—a large audience. Message on "In My Name Shall They Cast Out Devils," J.G.L. Testimonies revealed that during the week 5 men had been baptized in the Holy Ghost and spoke in tongues, also one woman.

MONDAY, NOVEMBER 28TH, 1910

At 4 p.m. I was called by Bro. Hunt to come to his home at once. A woman was in violent fits of insanity. I hastened to the home. As we prayed, the dear Lord cast out the insane devils, and when I left, she was lying quietly and preparing to sleep. It was a glorious deliverance. The Spirit came upon me, giving me a great and intense sense of dominion. Bro. & Sis. Hunt and Bro. Rothchild had been praying with her for hours

152

but had not sufficient dominion to cast the devil out, but being encouraged by my presence, prayed with great power. The Lord united our hearts in a great unity of faith. The woman's name was Farmer.

Monday night—beautiful conversion of a young man at tabernacle. The Spirit came on Bro. Scott Moffat. He had a beautiful vision of Jesus holding out His hands to him. Bro. Moffast is a Wesleyan local preacher.

TUESDAY, NOVEMBER 29TH, 1910

I visited Mrs. Dockrall's rooms at 56 Mosley building, Johannesburg, overlooking the market square.

The Duke of Connaught, with the Duchess and Princess Patrica were visitors in the city. The Duke was laying the cornerstone. Three thousand school children dressed in white occupied the bandstand and sang. About 1 p.m. we started downstairs to the restaurant. Mrs. Dockrall was in front and was down about 5 or 6 steps when she was seized with a violent spasm of pain. Her husband took her back to the rooms. I went down and ate dinner and returned to Dockrall's rooms.

As I started upstairs I was joined by Bro. Gordon Hinds. We found Mrs. Dockrall suffering violently. She was walking about, apparently quite insane. We tried to get her to permit us to pray for her, but she refused. Being persuaded she was not responsible for her actions, we took hold of her and prayed. As we prayed, she became prostrated by the Spirit, and we laid her on the bed. God answered, the violent suffering ceased, but there remained a considerable pain throughout the afternoon.

At about 6 p.m., as I prayed, the Spirit came upon me intensely. I could feel the Spirit flow down my arm and through my hand into her body. I was praying, and as I prayed, laid my hands on the afflicted part. She became calm; her pain ceased at once, and passed under the power of God. Jesus appeared to her and warned her to be brave and strong, that she was not yet entirely delivered, that her suffering would return. She remained free from pain and slept till 1 a.m. when her suffering returned with great violence.

In the morning, when I came out to breakfast, a telegram from Mr. Dockrall —

My home was at 4 Millbourn Rd., Bertrams, Jhburg, about 2 ½ miles from Dockrall's — said, "Helen had bad night. Come."

Signed Ben Dockrall.

I hastened down, prayed, again the intense suffering ceased. At 10 a.m. a most violent attack came upon her. She begged me to get her morphine and to bring a doctor, etc. I refused and fought the devil with all my power. At the end of 1 hour, I sent her brother-in-law to call the saints to prayer for her. At about 12 p.m., Mrs. Dockrall suddenly became conscious, turned to me as I knelt at her bedside and said, "The Spirit of the Lord is upon you," and instantly I realized it was. Again the healing virtue flowed through me. Again her pain ceased. Again Jesus came in a vision to her with a sword in His hand, fighting enemies.

She asked the Lord, "Why do you need a sword? Why do you have to fight?" The Lord said, "For you."

When the Spirit of God left her, the peace and glory of God remained upon her.

I called again at night with Bro. Powell and found her recovering.

NOVEMBER 30TH, 1910

At the tabernacle meeting, a widow lady, Mrs. Bovell, came in great distress knelt at the altar and cried, "My baby (about 1½ years old) is dying. Won't you pray? Won't you pray!" We all went to prayer.

The devil powers were very active. A mighty spirit of rebuke in the Spirit came on me. The baby was at Mrs. Freslick's home, 30 Lilian Road, Fordsburg. The doctor said it was poisoned, having eaten it somehow. We prayed. My spirit seemed to grapple with the devil. He was overthrown. I felt it, and as we arose, I said to her,

155

"Go on home, dear sister. Look up. Your baby is all right."

She begged me to come in the morning and I did, and found that as we prayed at the Tabernacle the night before—Nov. 29 & 30, 1910—the child had fallen sound asleep, was healed and well and walking about. Mrs. Bosman, Mrs. Freslick and myself knelt and gave thanks to God for His goodness.

THURSDAY, DECEMBER 1ST, 1910

Bro. Oliphant, native overseer, called to report the baptism in water of 17 native people at Vryheid, Natal, on Sunday, Nov. 27, 1910, also the consecration of 5 children.

Read letter from Bro. Sam Hulley, Cook House, C. C., telling of baptism in Holy Ghost of Bro. C. Watson and wife and another young lady, also of water baptism of 4 colored people, also of the baptism in water of Mrs. Hulley and baptism in H.G. of a sister—Robinson at Somerset E. C. C.

In the afternoon, I called on Mrs. Dockrall and found her almost entirely well, and we praised God. I then went to Krugersdorp, Mrs. Stuart was very anxious to see and talk with me concerning Mrs. Garmie, a woman at Randfontein, Central Holt, who was given up to die of cancer of the womb. The doctors said months ago they

156

could do nothing for her. She went to England for treatment, grew worse, and almost died on the return voyage. I had been to pray with her twice. Mrs. Stuart, Gordon Hinds, and Bro. Frisby also had been to pray for her. I felt the burden of her case rested on the saints at Kruegerdorp.

God answered prayer in great degree for her so that at different times 2 large sections of the cancer passed from the body. Mrs. Stuart will visit her today and bring me the last section of cancer, and I will have Dr. Willie examine it. God gave a wonderful spirit of prayer for her last night.

Friday, December 2ND, 1910

Came in from Kruegerdorp, where I had been all night stopped with Bro. & Sister Stuart and was greatly blessed by conversing with them. Our fellowship was sweet in God.

Attended court after dinner. James Mauselli charged by our tabernacle as a disturber of the peace, was discharged.

Saturday, December 3RD, 1910

Mrs. Stuart wired me to go to Randfontein Central Holt to see Mrs. Garmie and pray. Found her resting in God but had no assurance of ultimate victory for her healing. Bro. Vanderwall went with me and told me of a case of casting out of a devil that occurred at our tabernacle [in] Johnannesburg on Thursday evening last, when I was absent at Kruegerdorp. A man, a train conductor, said that a man appeared to him on the train, his own double, talked with him. At one station the double collected 7 tickets and brought them to him, and another 5 tickets. Then, together, they drank from a pint bottle of whiskey.

DEC. 3ᴿᴰ CONTINUED

The man was in great agony. Bro. Vanderwall, Sister Welsh, and Mrs. Vanderwall went into the back room, the vestry, and prayed for him. Bro. V.D.W. says he prayed several times commanding the devil to leave the man, when, suddenly <u>he left in a blue flame visible to all in the room</u> and disappeared through the door. Then the people rejoiced and praised God.

Dec.3rd, while on the train, we met Bro. Von Schele, who told us of meeting a woman Mrs. __ who was healed of inflammation of the lungs, double pneumonia, very bad.

Bro. and Sister V.D.W. and myself went to pray for her on Sunday, and she was greatly relieved. On Tuesday, Bro. V.D.W and myself went to pray for her and God entirely healed her. Bro. Von Schele had written a policy on her son-in-law's life and, while calling, the old lady told him how Jesus healed her. They were living with their daughter Mrs. __, Royal Cottages [Langlaagte?] Deep Mine.

Sunday, December 4th, 1910

Today was communion service in the morning at the Tabernacle. The Spirit of God was greatly present.

Among the testimonies, was one by a young Bro. Heroldt of Postchfish, for whom the church prayed about 2 weeks ago. He was run over by a cart and left unconscious was carried home. His wife would not have a doctor, but trusted God. Telegrams were sent to pray. God heard and answered. The doctors decided he must be operated on to remove the vast quantity of clotted blood, but he refused medical attendance altogether. His soul was overflowing with gratitude and instantly, upon giving his testimony, knelt down on the platform and invited the congregation to join him in a prayer of thanksgiving to God. A little child was prayed for who was ill of rheumatic fever. Mrs. Bovell, whose baby was healed when dying on Nov. 30, was present and praised God for the healing of her child.

Sunday, December 4th, 1910

Evening Service at Tabernacle

Two native men were present, a delegation from the Africa Catholic Church, consisting of the Bishop or moderator of their church and his chief advisor, who is a

159

grandson of the old Christian Barolong Chief, Morroco of the Jha Banchu O.J.S. They wanted to join our mission and receive the Apostolic Faith teaching. I spoke briefly on the general work of our mission, Bro. V.D.W. on the native work and the 18 churches these native brethren represented. And then Bro. Scott Moffat, a Wesleyan Methodist local preacher gave a striking testimony of how on the night of Nov. 28, at the evening service at the Tabernacle, the Spirit of God fell on him prostrating him on the floor for two hours, while the Lord showed him a beautiful stairway of wonderful architecture reaching from earth into infinitude and a beautiful figure in white floating down the stair (not walking) as he approached, he saw it was the Lord.

CONTINUED DECEMBER 4TH, 1910

There was a very fine evening audience. It is really wonderful how our audiences have kept up, considering how the devil through Cooper, Bowie, Gillis, etc. have tried to destroy the work.

MONDAY, DECEMBER 5TH, 1910

Monday at the night meeting a sister was converted. Her brother had been converted the previous Monday night. Spent day among the sick.

Tuesday, December 6th, 1910

Meeting at tabernacle in the evening. Terrible rain storm, only about 40 were able to be present. I was struck in looking over the audience to note how that most of them were real miracles of salvation and healing and how God uses the ministry of healing to get souls saved:

Davidson Brown, pianist & soloist, saved drunkard.

Peter Moffat, my bro-in-law (soloist), wonderfully healed.

Mrs. Jones, a rheumatic cripple, healed B.H.G. [Baptism in the Holy Ghost].

Mr. Jones, saved, drunkard.

Mr. Lind, who was an embezzler of a great sum of money from banks in Finland, who, when converted, confessed his sin and was forgiven. He used to come to my home, 4 Millbourn Rd., every Thursday evening for months for prayer. I only prayed and waited for God to deal with him. Bless God, He did. He was gloriously saved, has a fine position of trust, and is a most devout man. His wife was an invalid for many years, no medical aid would avail. Jesus healed her thoroughly as we prayed about 2 years ago.

Brother Welsh, a dear brother from Cape Town, raised in a Methodist family, who has been wonderfully baptized in the Holy Ghost & speaks in tongues. The glory of God rests on his soul.

Henry Dockrall, one of our workers, who was wonderfully saved from a vile life and baptized in the Holy Ghost. He told of how the dear Lord was using [him] and saving souls in his work at Boksburg North.

Rev. R. B. Vanderwall, a minister of the Dutch Reformed Church. He sinned, was expelled, became a drunkard, but Jesus saved him after we met him. He is now my chief assistant and secretary of the Apostolic Faith Mission executive council. God has wonderfully used him—saved and baptized in the Holy Ghost.

Mrs. R. H. Vanderwall, his wife, a miracle of the healing power of God, who was healed of God when in a state of coma after the drs. had given her up to die. She was prayed for and our Lord in His love healed her to the amazement of the doctors—Saved and baptized in H.G. Glory to God!

Maggie, Mrs. Vanderwall's daughter, who in my own home in June 1909, she was violently ill for a long time. After several weeks' illness, one night the death rattle came into her throat. She kissed her parents and brother goodbye. Then, as death came upon her, she roused and sang very faintly the first verse of "Jesus Lover of My Soul."

Jesus Lover of my soul

Let me to thy bosom fly

While the nearer waters roll,

While the tempest still is high.

Hide me, oh my Savior, hide

Till the storm of life is past

Safe into the haven guide

Oh, receive my soul at last.

As she sang, her voice died away, the death rattle ceased, her breathing apparently stopped, and so far as human judgment went, she seemed to be dead, and I have seen many die. As this went on, a strange operation was going on in my spirit. I seemed to see her leave the body and rise upward. She kept getting further away, very slowly. It seemed to me that I was holding her spirit by a grip of my spirit. The Holy Ghost was upon me in power.

After a time, I realized she was getting out of my control. I roused myself, prayed with more fervency, and finally, with command, I said, "You are not going away. In the name of Jesus Christ, come back." My spirit seemed to seize her and forcibly compel her return. Presently, I heard her mother say, "Oh, she is trying to breathe." Then, in a little while, she was breathing easily. God had heard. The blood-availed; Christ was conqueror.

On examination, we found she had been apparently dead 35 minutes. I have never felt free to say she was really dead, as there was no doctor present, but firmly believe if she had not been held by prayer, she would never have breathed again. Her spirit, I believe had already left her body. Today she is quite well and strong. I visited with her this evening and conversed with her about it. Praise to our loving Christ, she is saved and baptized in the H.G.

Mr. Jones, who had been a great drunkard, was present with his wife and sister-in-law. Since his conversion, he has been a dear, faithful brother, and his gratitude to God has been blessedly marked.

Mrs. Jones was a great sufferer many years of chronic rheumatism. Medical aid availed naught. Jesus impressed her to pray for her Baptism in the Holy Ghost. When she received the Spirit and spoke in tongues, to her own astonishment, she found also that God had healed her as she lay under the power of God on the vestry floor. The Lord made it plain to her to pray for the baptism and then she would be healed also. Bless God, Miss [Hirak], her sister, recently saved.

Miss Wick, my stenographer, saved and baptized in the Holy Ghost before I met her in America, when there in 1909. She came to Africa with me and has been a faithful stenographer and a good Christian worker. Many have been saved and baptized in the Holy Ghost under her ministry since she came. God bless her.

Bro. A. E. Sharpe, a dear brother, saved from drunkenness about 3months ago on the market square at an open air meeting. Now baptized in the Holy Ghost and preaching the gospel of Jesus Christ, especially to the natives at Brakpan.

His son, Bro. Sharpe, Jr.—saved and baptized in the Holy Ghost—a fine young worker.

G.H. Moore, a noble young miner. True to God and faithful worker in our mission. His testimony was a great blessing.

Wm. May, a young man who was saved and is now organist at Central tabernacle.

Scott Moffat, a Methodist local preacher, who is being led out into the deeper life in God, and whom God uses in the Word and Spirit to the salvation of souls. He had a wonderful vision of Jesus recently that has left a profound impression for good on his life.

Bro. Welsh, a Methodist brother, recently sanctified and baptized in the Holy Ghost, who is filled with the glory and praise of God. His life seems to be covered in the glory of Baptism in the Holy Ghost. He recently was given by the Lord a vision of Jesus coming in the clouds with myriads of angels attending.

John Guthrie, a precious brother in the Lord who is seeking God for a deeper life in the Holy Ghost.

Fred E. Mapstone, a dear young brother. Saved and sanctified and baptized in the Holy Ghost.

H.C. Birkigt, a dear brother, now caretaker of Central Tabernacle.

Mrs. Birkigt, his wife, people blessedly saved. In whose home many have been helped toward God.

Bro. E.E. Brink, a dear brother who related how that he had brought a young man to the Tabernacle who was afflicted with a guinea worm in his foot. Bro. Lake prayed for him saying, "Take off your shoe." It was in the foot and was said to encircle the foot 10 times in the flesh. When the worm was active, the torture was terrible. After prayer, he never felt it again. Jesus had killed it. The young man was a friend of Brink's. Through this, Brink himself was aroused and baptized in the Holy Ghost.

M.A. Cullinan, a lady worker in the mission, a devout woman formerly connected with the Salvation Army.

WEDNESDAY, DECEMBER 7TH, 1910

Called Parktown North just at time for a meeting. Called Bro. Powell to take the service and accompanied the messenger at Parktown South. We were met by Mrs. Gouse. Mr. & Mrs. Boswell, who accompanied me to a home where we found the woman had been seized with fits of violent vomiting. She had given birth [to] a child a few days previous. Her condition was very serious. The medical nurse who attended her was greatly astonished to see how [God] answered prayer for this woman, and it give a blessed opportunity to teach her of Jesus and His power to save from sin and heal from all disease. She pledged me to come and pray for other patients.

I remained at Mrs. Gouse's at Parktown North, and in the morning went to pray for a man, F. [Oushe?] sick of [inner] Phthisis, very bad. He had received partial healing when previously prayed for. His heart was very bad, and the left lung was very, very bad. His suffering ceased as we prayed, and he was immediately able to breathe down deep into the bottom of his lungs. He was very, very grateful to God.

THURS., DECEMBER 8TH, 1910

Returned to my home where I received my American mail. One letter from Bro. Studd contained an offering of $120. American currency (24 Guineas, English)

SUNDAY, DECEMBER 11TH, 1910

Morning service was a baptism service. 10 candidates— 8 European and then 2 native brothers who said they had come from far. I preached on baptism from Matt. 3. Bro. Vanderwall gave charge to candidates, Bro. Georgy Ulyate performed ceremony. Prayed for several sick at close of service.

MONDAY, DECEMBER 12TH, 1910

Worked at Miss Wick's office dictating letters till noon and at Mrs. Dockrall's office till night. Got out important letters for overseas mail.

TUESDAY, DECEMBER 13TH, 1910

Dictated letters during forenoon with Miss Wick. In the afternoon, I went to Mrs. Dockrall's, but the Spirit of God fell on us as we talked, and we spent most of the afternoon in meditation and prayer. Had a blessed time and God revealed to me his desire for an absolutely abandoned condition of our life to him, especially for one month with prayer and abstinence and meditation. The Holy Ghost promised to use us mightily.

The Spirit of God told her, Sis. Dockrall, to read the book of Nehemiah, about the manner of working on the walls—chap. 4:16 &17 was the special message. At night, my sister, Irene (Mrs. Moffat), who cares for my home, and I went to Jeppestown opposite the Jeppe School to pray for Mrs. Robt. Bruce—very sick of bloody flux. God touched her instantly as we prayed, and when we ceased praying, all pain had left her body. We returned at 10:30 p.m. God has been very near this afternoon. Praise His name. It has been a blessed day, nonwithstanding, I received a letter from Mrs. L. telling me that Mr. M. had charged me with the very vilest possible action to her at her house. Oh, blessed God, beloved, Jesus can take the sting out of our hearts.

Wednesday, December 14th, 1910

Received a splendid representative mail from 10 different points throughout the country giving news of the work—from Ladybrand, Africa, from Cape Town, Bloemfontein, Eastport, C. C., etc. and was much blessed in reading reports. Wrote a long letter to Bro.McClean of Jamaica, British West Indies. On calling Miss Wick, I learned that Bro. Welsh had been given liberty in tongues in language last night, also that Bro. Scott Moffat had received his Baptism in the Holy Ghost at his home last evening, for which I praise God. In the evening, I went to Boksburg North to open the new tent meetings there. There was a very nice audience, and God blessed.

Also two letters written from Africa by E. M. Scurrah to the saints throughout the world. These letters charge me with all vileness of misappropriation of funds, of all manner of evil machinations, etc. etc. But [none of] these things are worthy to be reckoned with in comparison with the knowledge of God through Christ Jesus our Lord.

Another letter from a Bro. Goss contained $5.00 from a Bro. Eaton of Winnipeg, Canada.

At the tabernacle service Thursday night, it was a very sweet service with nothing out of the ordinary. Mrs. Arlow of Wolhuter instantly healed of violent internal inflammation.

FRIDAY, DECEMBER 9TH, 1910

Worked at office. It was too wet at night for meeting at Fordsburg as arranged.

SATURDAY, DECEMBER 10TH, 1910

Worked at office, heavy rains preventing open-air meetings at night.

THURSDAY, DECEMBER 15TH, 1910

I have just had a call from Bro. Vanderwall, who told me that last night at the Central Tabernacle [Whburg?], while I was at Boksburg, that a woman was instantly healed of a paralyzed arm, as Bro. V.D.W., Bro. Scott Moffat, and Sister Hunt prayed for her at the close of the meeting. She said her arm was quite well and natural. Praise be to our God forever. Would that all men knew Jesus the healer.

I received today mail from Los Angeles, Cal., U.S.A,. containing copies of letters written by false brethren here. These letters had been sent world-wide denouncing me as all that was wicked and unholy. I also received a most unholy letter from one George Bowie, a man who apparently is or was a Christian worker of some kind but who seems to be consumed with envy or jealousy. This is the opinion of all the American brethren with whom I am closely associated, who assure of their confidence.

FRIDAY, DECEMBER 16TH, 1910

Spent the day dictating to stenographers getting out air mail. Nothing of more than ordinary interest occurred. Find myself suffering much from brain fray on account of overwork.

SATURDAY, DECEMBER 17TH, 1910

Still working on my mail for overseas. Received a beautiful letter from a Bro. Hoover, an American missionary stationed at Valpariso, Chile, South America, telling of God's revival there, of his people being baptized in Holy Ghost, etc., asking us to pray for his own and his wife's baptism. He says he has a Pentecostal assembly of 450 people.

SUNDAY, DECEMBER 18TH, 1910

Had a very sweet morning service. Bro. Vanderwall preached. In afternoon, I went to Simmer & Jack Hospital to pray for Bro. Jones, sick of double pneumonia. Had no evidence of immediate healing, but assurance that he would recover. Evening service was very blessed, large, splendid audience. Bro. Scott Moffat and Bro. Welsh were ordained as evangelists. A brother from Rustenburg was converted. Also prayed for a number of sick and the Lord healed them.

MON., DECEMBER 19TH, 1910

Dictated overseas mail all day. Did not go to evening meeting on account of weariness. Have been warned by the Holy Ghost of impending troubles coming soon. In conversation with Mrs. Dockrall, as we walked on the street, she said, "Oh, I feel as if the devil was working. The air is full of murder and suicide." At that very time, or half an hour after, a Mr. Bower shot his wife dead and then shot himself. Both of them were dead in a few minutes. The Holy Ghost continues to forewarn us of difficulty and trouble ahead.

Went to Crown Station and prayed for Mrs. Wentworth who was insane.

Tuesday, December 20th, 1910

Worked at office. Troubled because of lack of sleep from overwork. Had a meeting of our tabernacle ministry at our home in the evening. Had a pleasant social evening. God blessed us all very much.

Wednesday, December 21st, 1910

A very busy day.

Was called in company with Bro. Powell to pray for a Mrs. Mewbold of 26 Browning St., Jeepes, who was given up by the doctors. She had Bright's disease. As we prayed, God wonderfully touched her body, and she was instantly relieved of all pain and much blessed in her soul. Later I was called to pray for Mr. Geere at 20 Crown St., Jeppes, suffering from rheumatism all over his body but especially in his head and left shoulder. I laid my hands on his head and cast the devil out. As I ceased praying, I said, "Where is your pain?" He found it quite gone and praised and glorified God.

At the evening service, the dear Lord gave me a strong message from the entire 9th chapter of John on the healing of the blind man, his cowardly parents, his own testimony, Jesus found him after he was cast out of the synagogue, etc. A note was sent by Ben Dockrall telling me his wife was very ill. We found her suffering greatly with a violent headache and contraction of the spinal chord. As we continued to pray, the Lord instantly touched her. The chord relaxed, her suffering ceased, and she was well and praised God.

The Holy Ghost directed me to read, for my own comfort, Jeremiah 9th chapter, which I take to be a warning to the enemies of God's work, of his wrath upon them. I never knew such terrific malice and envy to exist before as is shown by Mr. Cooper, Mr. Bowie, Gillis, and others. Bro. Tom Hezmalhalch and I have peached together for several years, came together from America, but like Barnabas and Paul, now separate each to go his own way.

My heart is grieved and sore on account of his treachery, but feel it due to him to say it was the influence upon him of other false brethren, especially E. M. Scurrah, a stranger who ingratiated himself into Tom's good will, but who was a bold, vile man. His letters, written to America damaging my character and the character of others, have been returned to me. I never knew a professing Christian could do and write such things. How Satan has blinded their eyes. They cannot see God or His work for prejudice.

How frail we mortals be.

What patience God shows toward us all teaching us to be charitable with one another.

I bear no malice. Jesus won't let me. I only desire to go on my own way unmolested and pray God's blessings on them all through me.

In a letter from Bro. Henry Dockrall from Boksburg North dated Monday last, says, "The woman who was sick and who asked for prayer, the night you were here was healed when you, Helen, and Mendelsky laid hands on her." Praise God.

Mrs. Rensley of 13 Coywood St., Port Elizabeth, is visiting us for a time. She suffered with severe pain in her side for 3 years, and tells me that I prayed for her when I was at Port E. some months ago, and that she was entirely healed. To God be the glory.

Tonight at the Tabernacle service, Mrs. Jones of Gerriston, whose husband was sick of double pneumonia at the Simmer & Jack Mine Hospital, and for whom we prayed Sunday last, was present praising God for the marvelous healing of her husband last Sunday. She testified that about an hour after we prayed for him, the Spirit of the Lord came deeply upon him and his disease was gone.

God gave her a beautiful vision of her husband's healing to comfort her mind and heart and to assure her of his healing. She promised that she would send me a copy of it in writing.

A brother was baptized in the Holy Ghost at the meeting, as he sat in his seat. As he walked into the meeting, I burst out in speech to Miss Wick and others saying, "The Lord will baptize that man in the Holy Ghost tonight." During the service, he was baptized in the Spirit and spoke in tongues.

THURSDAY, DECEMBER 22ND, 1910

This is the second anniversary of my darling wife's death. Her maiden name was Jennie Stephens. We were married Feb. 5, 1891 at Millington, Ill., U.S.A. She was a loving, beautiful wife. Words can never tell all she was to me. God gave us a marvelous unity in the spirit. I worshipped her, and she me likewise. Oh I will ever forget when I returned from a missionary tour to find her already 12 hours dead. My precious wife. But as I look back over the terrible struggles of planting this work in Africa, I now really feel God in His mercy permitted her to escape this awful time of sorrow and trial and fighting by taking her to heaven. Lies, blackmail, suggestion of evil of every kind, they say I am possessed of a devil, that's how people are saved and healed, etc., etc. But Jesus heals the sick and saves the sinful every day, and this testimony of God baffles my traducers. They now openly say it is the devil who heals.

Friday, December 23rd, 1910

Received and interviewed workers from different parts of the field. Said good-bye to native ministers going to the Kronstad and other meetings. Helped them as I could with money for fares, etc. God has wonderfully helped me in this matter as many sent to me. He sent me 2 pound from a friend. When it was gone, Sister Dockrall gave me 2 pounds given by Bro. May of Randfontein Estates to her for me. So I have been able to put all our workers on the train. In the afternoon, the Council met the brethren of Vrededorp in joint council, at which time certain arrangements were made for to induce Bro. Thos. Hezmalhalch to bring forward signed charges of misconduct of the work of the mission, etc. and I agreed not to prosecute him in any court on account of the preferment of charges by him. Our thought was to arrive at the truhtfulness of these charges, and to make the way clear for him to come forward with same.

December 24th, 1910

Received Bros. Van Vurean and Van Jonder, evangelists. Bro. Van Jonder is a new man in our work. He was a prisoner of war in Ceylon. A Boer from Africa during the late Boer war, [he] was baptized in the Holy Ghost and spoke in tongues. On account of the Spirit of God resting upon him, he was thought to be insane and was sent to the hospital. Jesus revealed to him by a vision that in 9 years he would meet people who baptized by triune immersion and that he would be blessed and anointed of God to preach.

Sent a cablegram to my old Mother and Father at Sault Ste. Marie, Michigan, U.S.A. as follows: "Christmas Greetings. Lake, Moffats, everybody fine."

Went to cottage meeting at Van de Byls, Auckland Park, had a sweet time of communion, returned home at midnight.

Married 1891

My heart has been very lonely today. My thought was almost continuously with my dear wife in heaven. Oh, my darling, what dreary days since you went away. How I praise God for an active mind and body and plenty to do for others that has kept me busy and thereby kept my soul from being absorbed in the loss of you, my precious wife. You were all in all to me, and though now you have gone to God before me, I bless Him for the 17 years we were permitted to live together here and for our 7 beautiful children that God gave us.

Your memory is sweet. Today, every book, everything about me, speaks to me of you, my own lovely wife. But as a manly man, I can only go on and wait to meet you when my own time has come. And I must finish the work He gave me to do ere I can come to you. Our baby

Wallace who was only 18 months when you went away to heaven is now a fine boy of 3 ½ years.

And when you came, you swept the scale

    With a mighty master's wonderful art.

You made the minor keys sob and wail,

    While the low notes rang like a bell in a gale.

And every chord in my heart

    From the deep bass tones to the shrill ones above

Joined in that glorious harmony—Love

All happiness that human heart could know,

    I found with you.

And when you went away,

    The hours became a winding sheet of woe.

And make ghastly phantom of today.

But though the human is lonely,

    I yet rejoice my darling is with God

And sorrow not as those who have no hope,

But rejoice that the little while of parting

Will be over and we shall meet again.

SUNDAY DEC. 25TH, 1910 - CHRISTMAS

What memories sweep my soul today. Overwhelmed at the remembrance of my darling wife's death, I laid down and God permitted my tears to flow freely. As tears always do bring relief, it came. I went to the morning service and was rejoiced to receive a note from Bro. Henry Dockrall of Boksburg North, telling of the Baptism in the Holy Ghost of a young brother there. Bro. Townsend also told me of the Baptism in the Holy Ghost of a brother at Brakpan. Also, on Friday, Miss Horack came to tell me that she herself had been baptized in the Spirit on Friday at her own home as she prayed. I had noticed on Thursday night she was almost on the point of receiving the blessed Holy Ghost.

The brother from Vrededorp, who was baptized in the Holy Ghost at the Central Tabernacle Thursday night, makes 4 who where baptized in the H. G. that I know of this week. Bless God.

Mr. Stuart of Kruegersdorp also wrote me of the wonderful healing of Mrs. Wentworth, who was insane very bad, also sick from displacement of the womb.

We, Mrs. Dockrall and myself, went to Crown Station and prayed for her last Monday afternoon. She was very
180

bad. The devil seemed to have taken complete possession of her. As I approached her bed, she grew wild, saying, "Don't you pray for me. Don't you pray for me. I don't want prayer.

Don't touch me," etc. After a time, Sister Dockrall succeeded in getting her consent to let me put my hands on her head and pray. As I did so, the Spirit of God came upon me, and I knew the devil was instantly cast out. In a moment, she rose up in bed saying, "It's gone. Oh, praise God, it's gone!" Her husband and myself retired from the room, and Mrs. Dockrall then laid hands on the afflicted parts, and God healed her at once. She immediately arose and walked and continued well.

MONDAY, DECEMBER 2ND, 1910

Worked on mail overseas. In evening went to tabernacle. Received a request to come quick, Bro. Arlow at 33 Smit St., Bloemfontein. Took Mrs. D., called a cab and went fast. Found him suffering violently, apparently with extreme neuralgia. We prayed. The pain in body and head instantly ceased, but remained in one tooth. We prayed again, and I put my finger in his mouth on the bad tooth.

We prayed again. God stopped it right there. Then we went to Mr. Edwin Armms and prayed for Mrs. Armms' mother. She had a paralyzed arm, the result of an affliction of the glands of the throat. We prayed. Her suffering ceased, but not further evidence of healing came. The glands still remained hard, and the arm without power. We must go again. Something about her was not clear in the Spirit. I could discern it in the Spirit.

TUESDAY, DECEMBER 27TH, 1910

Took bundle of letters and papers to Mrs. D., then went to Bloemfontein to call on some of our people.

Found Mr. Arlow at home, said he had been well ever since we prayed. Had prayer with the family, after which Mrs. Arlow told me the following story of a remarkable healing: She said, "About 2 years ago, my brother-in-law and his wife and myself brought his sister, a Miss [Kotae], an imbecile and unable to speak, to the tabernacle. I prayed for her and instantly she commenced in tongues, and from that time on, she retained the power of speech.

About 2 months ago, the same 3 came to me after an evening service and asked me to pray for the deliverance of their sister, confined in the Pretoria Asylum. I said to them, "Let us stand here," (we were in the aisle). "Let us join our hands and hearts and God will deliver her."

The next day, her sister went to see her, and the authorities said, "She is suddenly well. We do not understand it, but she is well." Later, they signed her discharge, but just then her brother was killed in a dynamite explosion, and she had no place to go, so still remains at the institution." I purpose going to see her on my next trip to England.

I then visited Mrs. Phillis. Found her sick in bed. Prayed for her. God touched her. She had formerly been healed of internal tumor at the tabernacle. Her husband, who had been a great drunkard, was saved, and they have a happy home. Praise God.

Henry Dockrall from Boksburg North, has just called and tells me of the Baptism in the Holy Ghost of a Miss Scott this afternoon. Again, we praise Him.

WEDNESDAY, DECEMBER 28TH, 1910

Worked at Miss Wick's office in forenoon, at Mrs. Dockrall's office till 2 p.m. Called on Mrs. Vanderhoff and then took train for Boksburg. Meeting was in Mrs. Ward's home, the tent being wet. Four young people came and gave their hearts to God. Then the Lord baptized Mrs. Morgan in the Holy Ghost and she spoke in tongues. Then a man came forward and gave himself to God.

We had a blessed time—no preaching, the Spirit just fell on all. Some sang hymns

Bro. Kotze and Bro. Beattie were baptized in the H. G. at Harris' tonight while others prayed and testified. We returned to Johannesburg in a terrific rain.

Thursday, Dec. 29th, 1910

Worked at office. Received mail.

I notice Bro. George B. Studd of Los Angeles writes a strong endorsement of myself and work in <u>The Upper Room.</u> I received $96 in offerings from different ones in America today, for which I praise God. At tabernacle meeting tonight, an air of sadness seemed to weigh upon us. It was in the Spirit. Some were healed, and the Lord seems to be laying a burden of intercession on the people.

At the close of the meeting, Bro. Townsend introduced me to a young colored man who had been baptized in the Holy Ghost on Saturday night in the tabernacle vestry. Praise God.

Friday, December 30th, 1910

Prepare plans for all-night meeting. Instead of going to meeting at night, I went for a walk and finally went to a tea-room and conversed for a couple of hours with friends.

SATURDAY DECEMBER 31ST, 1910

Received workers from different fields coming to the all-night meeting: Bro. Saunders of Bloemfontein, Henry Dockrall, Mr. Morgan and wife, Bro. Scombie, Bro. Schuman of Middleburg, C.C., Bro. Scott Moffat, Bro. Welsh, and others.

We had a blessed all-night meeting, and the dear Lord gave a most blessed time, glorious time, and the Holy Ghost gave me a prophetic message outlining the progress of the work during the next years. At midnight, we had communion service, closing at 5 minutes to 12. Then we remained in prayer in silence as the clock struck 12. The meeting continued till morning.

SUNDAY, JANUARY 1ST, 1911

Had beautiful morning service. The Spirit of God was very manifest, the congregation was melted down in tears. Bro. Chas. Hately praised God for his wonderful healing of a diseased bone in his healthy head, for which there was no medical remedy, also for the healing of his right hand and forearm paralyzed by an accident, also for the healing of his leg. After a compound fracture, being permanently lame on crutches, the doctors gave him no hope of a cure. Jesus healed him, and his heart overflowed with gratitude. I do not know that I have ever listened to a testimony exhibiting a deeper sense of gratitude.

Evening service was a blessed time, and God called sinners to repentance. Four yielded their hearts to God and we all went home praising God for His love and mercy.

MONDAY JANUARY 2ND, 1911

Worked on overseas mail. Had a blessed time, indeed. Sent out a great many papers. At the evening service, 2 drunken men sought God for salvation.

TUESDAY, JANUARY 3RD, 1911

Prayed for man at Booysens Reserve in delirium tremens. Have never had to listen to such blasphemies. When I suggested I would pray for him, he cursed me in a terrible manner. His wife and cousin tried to quiet him. Finally, I went up to him, took his hands forcibly, and held him still. At the same time, I commanded him to look into my eyes. He did so. I put my face down within 6 or 8 inches of his, looking intently into his eyes. His gaze became fixed on my eyes, as mine were on his. Then, moving my hands, I laid them on his head, and in the name of Jesus Christ commanded the devil to come out of him. I felt it was instantly cast out. He became at once quiet and docile, turned on his face, and wept bitterly, praying God for salvation. It was a blessed experience, and I returned home praising God for his might power in delivering men from all the power of the devil!

WEDNESDAY, JANUARY 4TH, 1911

Oh soul on the highway from earth into glory,

Surrounded by mysteries and trial so near,

Let the light of thy God in thy life,

    be resplendent,

For Jesus will guide thee, thou need'st,

    never fear.

For if thou wilt trust Me,

    I will lead thee and guide thee,

Through the quicksands and deserts of life,

    all the way.

No harm shall befall thee, I only will,

    teach thee,

To walk in surrender with Me,

    day by day.

For earth is a school to prepare thee for glory.

The lessons here learned, you will ever obey.

THE HISTORY OF
JOHN G. LAKE HEALING ROOMS

The John G. Lake Healing Rooms were originally started in 1914 when Dr. Lake began teaching on the subject of Divine Healing in a local church in Spokane, Washington.

Dr. Lake rented a group of rooms in the Rookery Building that he converted into "Lake's Healing Rooms." He began praying for the sick on a daily basis and soon became so overwhelmed by the sheer numbers of those coming for healing that he was forced to train others in what he called "The Science of Divine Healing."

The people he trained were of various ages and were both men and women. They were taken through a "series of lectures" on divine healing that were designed to impart faith and knowledge to bring healing to the sick. The group of men and women that Lake trained were called Divine Healing Technicians. These technicians were trained daily by both teaching and hands-on practical application.

Upon completion of the training, they were given the name of a terminally ill patient and were told to go to them and stay with them, ministering to them until they were healed.

If they were not able to get the person healed, they were not to return to the Healing Rooms to continue in ministry. Dr. Lake had an ability to impart faith into his hearers.

He did this by teaching what he knew to be true from the Word of God concerning divine healing and the authority of the believer. Dr. Lake continued ministering in Spokane until 1920. From 1915 until 1920, the team of 16 Divine Healing Technicians and Dr. Lake recorded over 100,000 healings. Dr. Lake left Spokane in May of 1920 to go to Portland, Oregon, to begin a duplicate work there.

When Lake left Spokane, the Healing Rooms there ceased operating. When Dr. Lake returned to Spokane in 1931, he found that the work he had started no longer existed. He set about to re-establish a church and the Healing Rooms. Dr. Lake passed away in 1935 and the Healing Rooms never opened again. The original building that housed the Healing Rooms burned and a new building, bearing the same name and address was built on the same site. Dr. Lake never set foot in the new building.

In 1995 Rev. Curry Blake, General Overseer of John G. Lake Ministries, began plans to go to Spokane and reopen the Healing Rooms but was informed that the original building no longer existed. After a time of intense prayer and seeking the will of God, the Lord spoke and said not to focus on buildings and shrines but to carry the Spirit of the ministry.

In 1999, what is now called "Healing Rooms Ministries" opened in the <u>new building</u>. "Healing Rooms Ministries" at Spokane are NOT affiliated with John G. Lake Ministries nor are the teachings the same.

About the Author

Curry R. Blake was born in 1959 in Texas. Just before he was a year old he was accidentally run over by his father. His injuries were life threatening, but by a miraculous intervention his life was spared. Curry was  taught the Word of God by his Bible believing mother. In his early 20s he began to seek God concerning his calling.

He began ministering as opportunities came available in local Pentecostal churches. He avidly sought out information about those whom God had mightily used in times past. This eventually led him to South Bend, Indiana where he sat under the ministry of Lester Sumrall. Later, after the tragic passing of his daughter, he came in contact with Wilford Reidt, the son in law of John G. Lake. Reidt recognized that Curry fulfilled a prophecy given by Lake concerning his successor, so prior to his death he passed John G. Lake Ministries over to Blake.

In the mid-90s Blake was given a manual used by John Lake to train his Divine Healing Technicians. With this new found information Curry pursued the healing ministry with new vigor. This time the results were staggering!

Within five years time he was traveling across the United States praying for the sick and training literally thousands to heal the sick. His ministry is currently located in Dallas, Texas where Curry is training a new generation of miracle workers through the Dominion Bible Institute.

You can learn more about Curry Blake and John G. Lake Ministries by visiting: www.jglm.org

John G. Lake Ministries
SAME MESSAGE. SAME POWER. SAME RESULTS.

PARTNER WITH US AS WE ADVANCE GOD'S KINGDOM ON EARTH!

Partner Benefits Include:

- Our monthly "Laboring Together" newsletter with a ministry update directly from Brother Curry that includes detailed information about our upcoming events and activities. We compile testimonies from all over the world to encourage and strengthen your faith.

- Partner E-Newsletter includes an MP3 every month taught by Brother Curry with the option to download our monthly audio teaching.

- 30% Discount on all products during the holiday season...

- Our Promise to Protect Your Kingdom Investment.

Partners can choose to receive packets by postal mail or via email. Your faithful support allows us to help give our materials away freely to those who cannot give, such as our JGLM prison ministries, disaster relief funds and foreign missionaries. Most importantly we depend on our faithful partners as our main line of prayer support.

Email: partners@jglm.org
www.jglm.org/partners

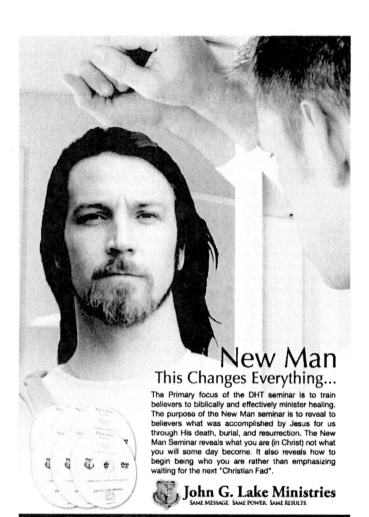

New Man
This Changes Everything...

The Primary focus of the DHT seminar is to train believers to biblically and effectively minister healing. The purpose of the New Man seminar is to reveal to believers what was accomplished by Jesus for us through His death, burial, and resurrection. The New Man Seminar reveals what you are (in Christ) not what you will some day become. It also reveals how to begin being who you are rather than emphasizing waiting for the next "Christian Fad".

John G. Lake Ministries
SAME MESSAGE. SAME POWER. SAME RESULTS.

The Teaching That Birthed A Legend Is Now Raising An Army.

DOMINION LIFE
INTERNATIONAL
APOSTOLIC
CHURCH

Glory to God, Freedom for All!

Church Membership Requirements

1. Must confess Jesus as Lord and that you are saved and born again.

2. Must at least be seeking and expecting to be filled with the Holy Spirit in accordance with Acts Chapter 2 (speaking with other tongues).

3. Must agree with the JGLM/IAC Statement of Faith, obtained by emailing us at: dliac@jglm.org.

4. You agree to pray for us according to the prayer directives that we will send to all church members on a regular basis.

5. You agree to support the church through tithes and offerings. Tithes and offerings must be sent to the church address and MUST be noted as Tithes/Offerings.

6. You agree to work towards becoming a certified DHT. Our hope is that ALL DLIAC members work toward becoming a certified DHT to advance the kingdom through this body. For information on becoming a DHT contact us by email at: iac@jglm.org or you can find all information on our website at www.jglm.org.

7. You agree to remain in the unity of the Spirit by living a life in accordance with the constitution and bylaws of the I.A.C.

John G. Lake Ministries
SAME MESSAGE. SAME POWER. SAME RESULTS.

DOMINION
BIBLE INSTITUTE
TRAINING THE NEXT GENERATION OF GOD'S GENERALS

SIGN UP TODAY!
dbi@jglm.org

John G. Lake Ministries
SAME MESSAGE. SAME POWER. SAME RESULTS.

- You are left unsatisfied by the status quo...
- You know you were meant to be a participant and not just a spectator...
- You ask "Why not?..." more than "Why?"...
- You believe that today can be better than yesterday...
- You know you were meant to walk among the Giants of the Faith, and you want the tools & training that can make it happen...
- When you hear the exploits of God's Generals, you can picture yourself doing them...

If this describes you, then you ARE JGLM... whether you know it or not.

COME.
LET'S CHANGE THE WORLD.

 John G. Lake Ministries
SAME MESSAGE. SAME POWER. SAME RESULTS.

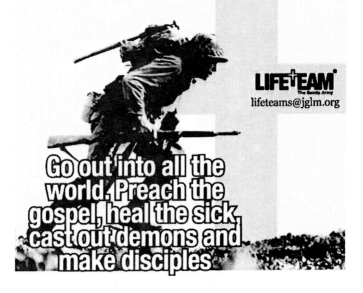

LIFE TEAM
The Saints Army

lifeteams@jglm.org

Go out into all the world. Preach the gospel, heal the sick, cast out demons and make disciples

JGLM Trademarked Names

Divine Healing Technician(s)
John G. Lake Ministries
John G. Lake Healing Rooms
John G. Lake's Divine Healing Institute
Dominion Life International Apostolic Church
Dominion Bible Institute

All derivatives of these names are Copyrighted trademarks and may not be used without the express written permission of:

John G. Lake Ministries
P. O. Box 742947
Dallas, Texas 75374
www.jglm.org

Please advise JGLM if you come into contact with anyone using the following names without authorized permission:

John G. Lake Ministries
John G. Lake's Divine Healing Institute
John G. Lake Healing Rooms
Divine Healing Technicians Certified
DHT